# My Holding You Up Is Holding Me Back:

## Recovery From Over-Responsibility And Shame

Joy Erlichman Miller

Health Communications, Inc.
Deerfield Beach, Florida

Joy Miller
Renewal
Peoria, Illinois

**Library of Congress Cataloging-in-Publication Data**

Miller, Joy Erlichman
    My holding you up is holding me back: recovery from over-responsibility and shame / Joy Miller.
      p.    cm.
    Includes bibliographical references.
    ISBN 1-55874-091-0
    1. Adult children of dysfunctional families — Psychology. 2. Responsibility. 3. Shame. I. Title.
    RC455.4.F3M54                    90-32329
    158'.24—dc20                     CIP

© 1991 Joy Erlichman Miller

ISBN 1-55874-091-0

Publisher: Health Communications, Inc.
              3201 S.W. 15th Street
              Deerfield Beach, Florida 33442-8190

*Design by Graphic Expressions*

# Acknowledgments

With each new book, I have rejoiced in pondering the credits and acknowledgments. I loved this point in my writing because it allowed me the opportunity to express my inner emotions openly to those I loved and appreciated in my life — and I do love talking about feelings! As I wrote this third book, however, I found it interesting that I never thanked or acknowledged the one person that I truly loved and trusted. How could I have been so neglectful? Was it my fear of what people would say? Today I acknowledge and celebrate publicly this wondrous person in my life: *me.*

*Joy:* I thank you, Joy, for holding my strength within, and for keeping my eyes clear to see the love and splendor of life. I rejoice in the safety I have found within my being. Each day is filled with intensity and an amazing rush of emotions when I am with you. You have allowed me to experience the gift of humor and the ability to never lose my inner child, who is safely embraced by my wondrous Playful One. You find love and beauty in all you see, as you always look for the positive aspect of everything! I have loved you for letting me really feel "in the now" and not returning back to the numbness that held me captive for so long. I embrace my progress and my journey Home.

In the darkness I could not see, but thankfully I did dare to look. I am a beloved child of the universe and today I do know that *I am enough!* I have come such a long way. I now feel free to be open, vulnerable and trust my inner voice. I believe in my process and truly am learning to be my own best friend.

*Heidi:* Asleep for so long, you yearned to see the real me. You looked in my eyes and dared me to be with me. Scared and fearful, as I was, you created a safe harbor for our miraculous friendship. You gave me the gift that you had protected for so long — the freedom to be with your real inner child. So long ago we spoke of you as a gorgeous unopened present, a gift of love for those who dared to look deep inside. I am so fortunate and grateful that you shared your gift with me. Destiny brought us together and our love will keep "us" strong and safe. You are a part of me, and no words can express my love and gratitude for you truly were the one who led me to myself and all I could truly dare to be. N & E, Little Ducky!

*Josh:* Oh, how we have grown, my son. We have shared the joy, the sorrow and the ecstasy of each day. My son, you are my greatest joy as I watch you grow. I smile and rejoice in listening to you share your deepest feelings and become open to being all that you can be. I am so very fortunate to have you in my life. You are more than I could ever have wanted or dreamed. You fill my heart with splendor when I look into your big blue eyes. They are the windows to your heart, and through them I see how loving and wondrous you truly are. Please remember as you journey down your path that I am always here with my arms open, waiting to embrace you. Love yourself and nurture your inner growth. You have only the limits you set for yourself. I believe in you. My son, my son, my kingdom for my son. I will always love you, Boober!

*Rhonda, Pam:* You were always there . . . you listened and listened and listened and helped me see my Truth. You dared to share your own special gifts of love with me. I could not have asked for any dearer friends. You are gifts of love and I am so thankful that we are walking "home" together.

*John:* Together again. You have walked on the path, meeting me at another crossroad. We have learned so much and gained only our strength and love. What we learned was worth the road that diverged in the forest and brought us into our new place. We have been able to bridge our pain and heal our wounded inner child in the safety of each other. I love you "wazoolions."

*Flip:* My dear friend, what would I have done without you? Your honesty and nurturing love has filled my heart with the gift that *only you* could give. Together we have grown and celebrated our journey in a vital part of our daily life! You are the brother I never had and I thank the universe for you. My love, DC!

*Dottie:* Your words help me express what is pouring out of my heart. What would I do without your editing and your personal visions of insight, growth and recovery? You are a wondrous gift in my life. I have watched you grow and mirror my own pathway. You have my love and appreciation!

*Sharon and Phyllis:* Thank you for your expertise with editing and your constant support in my career. You are dear friends in my life.

*Clients and Friends:* So many of you have shared your recovery from shame and over-responsibility. We have learned from each other in so many ways. Thank you for trusting me with your wounded inner child. I value your trust, support and love.

*Mom and Dad:* Please know that you were the ones who taught me to love. We all have issues we must address. This book illustrates my struggle. Without you I would not have learned how to persevere, nor how to celebrate my successes and laugh along the way. My love.

*My Extended Family at Health Communications:* I'm so fortunate to have so many gifts of love in my life. Special thanks to Gary and Peter who have always supported me; Marie, Luanne, Vickie, Suzanne, Michael and Milena who have been my friends; Randy, Eileen, Diane G., The Nerb, Jay, Karen, Andy and, of course, Ade.

My supportive family at the U.S. Journal who have assisted my spiritual and personal growth — with gratitude and love to Ruthie Fishel, Jane Middelton-Moz, Pat O'Gorman, Jerry Florence, Marilyn Volker, Rob Becker, Wayne Kritsberg, John Lee, Mary Lee Zawadski, Roxie Lerner and Carla Wills-Brandon.

*Over-responsibility:* a co-dependent action in which we overextend ourselves and become responsible for the actions, feelings or situations of others. This behavior is not limited to accountability for matters that concern our own behavior; it is a dysfunctional, self-destructive need to caretake for others. Over-responsibility is generally a learned response we use to gain approval, increase self-esteem or promote dependency. Sometimes we become over-responsible in the hope of meeting our perceived expectations of others.

*Shame:* a painful feeling of guilt, embarrassment or disgrace that affects our basic core. Shame says we are inherently defective. Shame refers to our internal selves, not to how we behave in a certain situation. Shame can create self-abandonment and self-dehumanization, and diminishes our self-worth and self-esteem.

# Introduction

I always believed that I was required — no, mandated — to be responsible for everyone in my life. My over-responsible behavior was my way of showing respect, love and care. If I really loved someone, I would do *anything* for them; the outpouring has no limits. Devotion equals action, and that means being everything for someone. If I could accomplish this goal, I felt, then I would surely control my destiny and people would love me and view me as worthy. Then the emptiness would be filled deep inside my core and I would know that I was enough!

For 37 years I proceeded along this path, lost to myself but responsible to the world. The good little Joy . . . dead inside except for the temporary "fixes" I got when I took care of others. Holding others up held me back, but I couldn't (or wouldn't) see it. I looked good to everyone else but I felt so bad!

Finally I reached a place where I could no longer survive (I certainly wasn't living). I began to listen, to learn, and I boldly took a step into the new direction I feared: change. The boat rocked; people scolded and shamed me for my new direction. I tried desperately to explain. I pleaded and bargained in the hope of gaining their acceptance. But soon I realized only *I* could give myself the acceptance I needed.

Controlling and over-responsibility lock us into expectations, disappointment, pain and shame. But, as we all must eventually discover, we are powerless over our behavior and must surrender. Surrender can be frightening, as I know. I still feel out of control sometimes without my over-responsible behaviors. I still have nightmares that others will discover my inadequacies and leave me.

Nevertheless, I have found glimpses of serenity along my path. I have discovered what I can change and where I must let go and release. I am recovering from over-responsibility and the shame that binds my inner child. I hold on to hope and witness my strength and self-nurturing. I celebrate my successes daily. I am stronger and I am beginning to see the Light.

I have learned that one of my most healthy recovery tools is celebrating and encouraging my positive attributes. I used to believe that criticism and judgment were the only mechanism for change in my life. But now my inner voice speaks gently to me and I listen to her encouragement. I see my progress. I am accepting and claiming my power while I focus on my journey. I have learned that trying to control others only harms my soul and fills me with obsession and anguish.

I know I am not alone — many of you are potential change-makers. For too long you have taken for granted the fact that you are a wondrous miracle! The following pages contain stories of other men and women who mirror what you feel deep within. Their stories reflect parts of yourself that you have fought to deny. The fact that you are reading this book means you are ready to break denial and capture your own power. Also included are over 50 suggestions for healing the hold of our over-responsible patterns. These hands-on ideas are included to assist your search for healing the shame that holds you powerless. You will find a suggestion section at the end of each chapter heading.

I am no master. I only hope to facilitate your journey as we all take the pathway toward our enlightenment.

*Joy Erlichman Miller*

# Contents

# Over-Responsibility Inventory

*Please answer YES or NO.*

_____ 1. Do you generally put other people's needs ahead of your own?

_____ 2. Do you generally see things that need to be done and take on the challenge without someone asking?

_____ 3. Do you have difficulty sleeping and relaxing because you find yourself mentally obsessing about things that need to be done?

_____ 4. Do you have difficulty saying "no" and establishing personal boundaries?

_____ 5. Do you lose yourself in relationships?

_____ 6. Do you find that you often do not live up to your own expectations and goals?

_____ 7. Do you feel worthy only when you get the approval of others?

_____ 8. Do you have difficulty celebrating your successes or seeing your accomplishments?

_____ 9. Do you often find yourself physically, emotionally and spiritually tired?

_____ 10. Do you have difficulty expressing your true needs, wants and desires?

_____ 11. Do you feel as if no one appreciates what you do and therefore everyone takes you for granted?

_____ 12. Were you the family caretaker in your home of origin? Do you see yourself now as a fixer or caretaker?

_____ 13. Do you believe you are "not enough" in your basic core?

_____ 14. Do you derive your self-worth and self-esteem generally from sources outside yourself?

_____ 15. Do you believe that the best way to get something done is to do it yourself?

If you have answered YES to more than five questions, then you probably feel over-responsible for others in your life.

For many of us over-responsibility is a debilitating and de-structive addiction that cripples our ability to care for ourselves and our needs. In an attempt to gain what we did not have in our homes of origin, we seek approval and worth from others. Internally we continue to struggle against accepting that we are enough and worthy.

We have become our own Critical Parent and carry this fault-finding, judgmental person inside at all times. This inner critical voice keeps us from listening to our true inner voice and also keeps us distant from our Higher Power.

It is imperative that we become aware of the internal pres-sures and demands that are pulling on us. Much of our over-responsibility is a product of our "shoulds" — our internal expectations — and the need for approval in an attempt to "do it right."

Just as taffy is pulled and stretched in many opposing direc-tions, we have allowed ourselves to be manipulated in an attempt to prove our worthiness. These pulls stretch us thinner and thinner in effectiveness and consistency.

One way to discover your internal pulls is to do the follow-ing exercise (see Figure 1). In the empty space next to the drawing of the overburdened person, write the messages — of people, places, things or expectations — that "demand" that you become over-responsible. Use the space to explore the "shoulds" or pulls placed upon you by friends, parents, relatives, spouse, primary relationship, job and religion, as well as your home-of-origin messages.

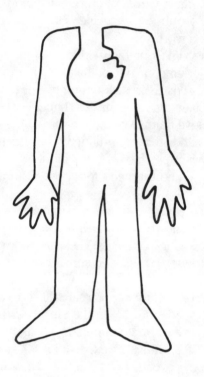

**Figure 1. Your Over-Responsibility Burdens**

*If you don't change directions,*
*you may end up where you are going.*

— *Lao Tse*

*Insanity is truly expecting different*
*results from the same behavior.*

— *Ruth Fishel*

# Do You Generally Put Other People's Needs Ahead Of Your Own?

"Practically perfect in every way" are the words Mary Poppins used to describe herself to the bewildered children in P. L. Travers's books, *Mary Poppins.* Her mysterious floating umbrella brought her to 17 Cherry Tree Lane in London, England, to work as Nanny to Jane and Michael Banks. This was the bizarre entrance of a woman whose career exemplified living life with the viewpoint of putting everyone else's needs before her own.

Mary Poppins miraculously arrived at the home of four people who desperately needed her fixing. This curious magical visitor saw the opportunity to change lives with her caretaking. She always lived her life in accordance with the philosophy of taking care of families in need of her service. Being a Nanny was not just a job for Mary, it was a way of life! Her over-responsible behavior changed the lives of others but left her in servitude until she felt her task was completed, then off she went, umbrella raised on high. But . . . not everyone has such a magical umbrella . . .

My home of origin strongly encouraged me to put the needs of others first as an act of love and caring. Unfortunately I never learned to find a balance between caring for others and caretaking. I believed the more I loved, the more I *should* caretake. The word "should" is an important element in this self-destructive behavior, because I felt that this was my *only* acceptable behavior. But my respectful, giving and caring behavior was clearly correlated to over-responsible co-dependent patterns.

I lost the ability to realize and state my needs and wants. In high school I followed the lead of others because I wanted their approval and validation. Besides, I had no idea of what I heard inside — my inner voice was locked away and inaudible. Adding to the destruction, I believed women should always be passive and do what others wanted. I feared that listening to my own needs would cause a chaotic situation and open the door to rejection. To protect myself from abandonment I *always* put others first. I usually went to extremes with the misguided belief that the more I did for others, the more they would love me. This error in my thinking was quite a set-up: an only child who became responsible for everyone around her in an attempt to feel like she was enough.

A client named Tom learned the same lesson in his home of origin, but he *had* to be responsible. His alcoholic mother's emotional and physical absence left him alone to care both for her and his baby sister. His mother made numerous suicide attempts and his father told him that Tom was the only one who could keep his unstable mother from taking her life. Tom felt as if he had no choices or options. What else could he do except be responsible for everyone else's needs? If he didn't put others first, he would surely be responsible for his mother's death and his sister's loss of her mother.

Another client, Ken, couldn't figure out why people never became close to him emotionally. It was obvious that he cared for the significant others in his life. He always listened and tried to help his loved ones in any way he could. Ken would stay up into the wee hours, listening to everyone else's problems and painful situations, offering loving support and expressing empathy. It wasn't that he didn't have significant issues in his own life, but somehow his needs were never as important or imperative as those of his friends. Of course he hurt inside, but a real friend helps others when they are in need. Responsible people are there for those who need support. Ken believed it was selfish to say "no" or not be available for his loved ones. He believed that he must put his pain aside when others needed him so desperately!

Ken was a prisoner of his own design. By cementing his feelings deep within, he had become emotionally frozen. His over-responsibility demanded that Ken live vicariously on others' feelings, and this destructive behavior kept him hopelessly locked in over-responsibility and shame. Subconsciously Ken had chosen to be responsible for others so he would not have to risk being responsible for his own life. This process enabled him not to face his own feelings and pain and protected him from feeling his emotions. He was controlling his life, but it kept him emotionally dead.

During a therapy session Ken reconstructed the dynamics of his home of origin. As he looked back Ken remembered how he had been taught at age three to be attentive to all of his aging grandmother's needs. She was frail and had very few people who were available to hear her daily aches and pains. Ken's parents told him that it was his "responsibility" to listen patiently and care for his grandmother. Because of her failing health he knew he *should* be giving, which meant doing whatever she requested and listening to everything she wanted to discuss. Ken learned that his focus should be directed outside himself and that it was his job to be the friend in grandma's life. Young Ken, however unfair, was to be responsible for his grandmother's emotional well-being. Ignoring his responsibility meant that he was shameful and selfish.

"She was so very old and so lonely," he said. "My family had some strongly engrained traditions. The most pervasive rule was that I was expected to respect my elders and put them first. It was my *duty* to be kind, sensitive and giving to her. She deserved it and expected it. I guess I learned to relate to everyone in the same fashion. My role is to be everyone's best friend and confidant, even if it is at my own expense."

## SUGGESTION:
## Playing Your Own Game

Bill, a wondrous man who is incredibly dedicated to his recovery, shared a televised interview he watched with the great tennis legend Billie Jean King. She repeated the advice she frequently gives to her peer and friend Martina Navratilova. Her four easy-to-remember quotes are a concise guideline not only for tennis, but for recovery from over-responsibility, as well as giving us the skills for self-loving. You will find these recommendations an excellent integration tool for daily life:

1. Slow down.
2. Keep your eye on the ball.
3. Stay in your own court.
4. Play your game.

### 1. Slow Down

As you slow down you will learn to *respond* rather than react to others. Reacting is an automatic habitual action caused by a stimulus; responding on the other hand, is an action you take after listening to your inner voice.

Slowing down teaches you that you have options and that they deserve to be acknowledged and considered. Take a good look at your needs, wants and desires and carefully consider your options. *Then* choose the best course of action.

This process will give you freedom of choice, the safety of time, inner guidance and self-nurturing. It is essential to allow yourself the time that you need to make responsible, healthy decisions. Your home-of-origin training taught you to feel the urgent need to make decisions on the spot, but they may not be the best decisions. How many times have you wished that you had given yourself adequate time to make sensible decisions that were in *your* best interest? Slow down.

### 2. Keep Your Eye On The Ball

As you learn to keep your mind (and heart) "on the ball," you will begin to pay attention to the issue at hand. Look at the present circumstance and don't let other issues, old shame messages and past habitual behavior distract you from your path.

My dear friend and fellow author Ruth Fishel taught me a lesson about my personal recovery. Ruth instructed me to put my arms straight out in front of my body and then touch my palms together. "This is your path, Joy — walk straight ahead. If you veer off the road, you will lose your way. If you look to the side for too long, you will begin to be distracted and your arms will begin to pull apart."

Ruth explained that I tended to be distracted by all the things and people along the road and thus I would lose sight of where I was headed. I tended to get so caught up in the surrounding issues, I let less important things keep me from my path in my recovery. Many times I get caught in my habitual co-dependent behavior and veer off the road because I am looking down other people's pathways. When the environment becomes the focus, I lose my route to recovery. I generally start to get caught up in the surroundings and begin to defend the "whys" of my journey and lose my energy in that way.

Remember to keep your eye on the ball — that is, on where you are going. Learn to keep your eye on the ball and your pathway clear of obstacles.

## 3. Stay In Your Own Court

When you caretake, you are playing on the other side of the net. It is as if you invaded the other person's boundaries and grabbed the racket out of his or her hand. Your focus person may be shocked at first, but eventually he or she concedes and gives you the racket. Now you are playing the game with yourself! You believe in your heart that you are helping, but you are only running back and forth across the net like a chicken with its head cut off. You sweat, you groan, you whimper — but you do continue the match!

Finally, exhausted and frustrated you discover that you are sabotaging your own needs, wants and desires. The focus person actually sits on the sidelines criticizing or judging your performance. You are outraged!

"How can they be criticizing me?" screamed an adult child of an alcoholic (ACoA) named Sue Ellen. "I did it all for them and this is my reward — their complaining and contempt! No matter what I do, it appears I never do it right. They all are so irresponsible and I have no choice but to take care of them. Is that what I get in return?" Sue Ellen had not yet discovered that she was taking care of someone else's recovery (and growth) at her own personal expense, as well as robbing the other person of the advantages of self-caring. Stay in your own court!

## 4. Playing Your Own Game

In the past you always matched your game with that of your focus person, like a mime who has learned to mimic how others live life. Then, using this ability to transform your life, you created a situation in which you could be a clone of the other person instead of being the genuine, authentic *you*.

To change you must learn to play your own game. Your game plan is to become aware of your needs, wants and desires and to be considerate of your own recovery plan. Being real with yourself is the most vital part of self-loving and self-nurturing. When you mimic others, you will always be out of sync with yourself. Play your own game!

These four rules can become guidelines for your healing process. They are a strategic plan for reclaiming your personal growth. Just as each stroke of the tennis racket is one step toward match point, your recovery must also be one step at a time. But you are not alone. Together we are striving to approve and affirm our journeys as we recover from the shame of over-responsibility and co-dependency.

*Today I am learning to care
for myself in a loving fashion.
I am nurturing and reparenting
my inner child with love
and understanding. I am a
beloved child of the universe.
I am enough.*

# Do You Generally See Things That Need To Be Done And Take On The Challenge Without Being Asked?

Gotham City was vigilantly protected from villains by the ever-present protectors: Batman and Robin, the Boy Wonder. These two miraculous defenders would rush unasked into dangerous and traumatic situations and rid the defenseless city of all wrongdoers. The dynamic duo was always on guard, awaiting any crisis!

Clearly their lives were dedicated to caring for others in need. Obsessed with their protecting role, the twosome dedicated their efforts to fixing and solving chaos — usually without being asked.

It is interesting to note that Bruce Wayne, Batman's alter ego, went virtually unnoticed without his heroic disguise. As Bruce Wayne he was dull, humdrum and boring. As Batman, he was glamorous, powerful and admired by everyone. Without his caretaking behaviors Bruce was just an ordinary stuffed-shirt millionaire who was incapable of living life to its fullest.

Boy Wonder Robin was so invisible that we only knew he was the ward of Bruce Wayne — he didn't even deserve to have a last name! Robin, abandoned by his family, dedicated his life to caring for everyone else. Perhaps both men were brought up in dysfunctional families where co-dependency was rewarded.

As a child hypervigilance was my middle name. I mastered the skill by the age of 10. Constantly aware of everyone else's needs, I would survey any situation and take action. My goal was always to assist everyone around me in order to gain their approval. If I became proficient in my over-reponsible behaviors, I told myself, I would never be abandoned. How could anyone reject such a giving person?

When I was in my 30s, a dear friend remarked that she never felt able to give to me emotionally because I always did everything before anyone else had a chance to act.

"I feel so deficient and inadequate and just want to help you out. Just once! Who could ever feel responsible in your presence? I always feel so irresponsible!" I looked at her with amazement. I did feel neglected and somewhat disappointed that she (and everyone else) didn't treat me the way I treated them. I did not realize I had made it impossible.

Facing the fact that I did not allow others to be responsible for their own behavior was only one facet of this over-responsible puzzle. I later came to realize that my hypervigilant behavior was also a means of control. (That word still turns my stomach, just as it did the first time I realized it was a part of me.) If I accomplished a deed for someone before they asked, I thought I could control how they viewed me. If I could control the outcome, then I might be rewarded and praised for my concern and caring. My actions were a means of controlling my unpredictable environment. I felt this behavior added a layer of padding in relationships — but I was wrong.

## SUGGESTION:
### Behavior Inventory

Use the following questions as a quick inventory to investigate your behavior patterns. The information will help you understand the basis of your behaviors.

What do you lose by being over-responsible for others?

1. _____

2. _____
3. _____
4. _____
5. _____

What keeps you from taking the risk of being self-responsible?
1. _____
2. _____
3. _____
4. _____
5. _____

What might you gain if you choose to look at new options and become self-responsible?
1. _____
2. _____
3. _____
4. _____
5. _____

As you search for new options in your life, please remember that every small change needs to be rewarded. Be gentle with yourself and notice that you are making progress along your path. As you continue your journey it is important to you to nurture yourself with the same loving, supportive care that you have always given to others. *This* time rejoice in giving love to yourself.

## SUGGESTION:
## STOP

Try the STOP technique *(Stand Tight On Proceeding)* to learn to respond rather than react. Reacting implies that you take an action immediately after you sense a need for action

— as when you see an opportunity to be responsible, ignore your own needs and inner voice and plunge in.

Responding is quite different. You still may sense a need for action, but you allow yourself time to consider your needs as well as the needs of others before you proceed. This process will allow you the opportunity to witness your automatic caretaking and over-responsible behaviors.

When you see something that needs to be done, STOP and repeat those four words to yourself: *Stand Tight On Proceeding.* Practiced regularly, this mental intervention will help you decide if you are being responsible to yourself first.

*Today I am becoming more understanding of my self-destructive patterns and am making positive changes in my life. I am a beloved child of the universe. I am enough.*

# Do You Have Difficulty Sleeping And Relaxing Because You Find Yourself Mentally Obsessing About Things That Need To Be Done?

The jungles of India hold many tales, but none is as famous as the story of Mowgli the Mancub who was found in a basket by a riverbank. Discovered by a nurturing black panther named Bagheera, the baby was taken to a wolf family in the hope that they might parent the child. Despite the differentness of this human creature, the wolves acquiesced to Bagheera's pleas and agreed to raise the child as one of their own. But fear entered the wolf pack with the rumors that the dreaded tiger, Shere Kahn, was nearing their community. Rumors turned to terror and soon the pack firmly believed that the man-eating tiger, Shere Kahn, would enter their peaceful village to kill the Mancub and all who protected him.

For days and nights the wolf elders discussed the potential harm that might come if they continued to protect the Mancub whom they loved as one of their own. They battled with the difficult decision and their over-responsibility for the young lad, who was now quite capable of protecting himself in the jungle. The wolves who loved him so dearly treated him much differently than their own cubs. Elders always taught cubs about their rite of passage, and the need for self-sufficiency in the jungle. But the wolves were fearful of surrendering their hold on Mowgli, which kept him childlike and irresponsible.

Many nights I lay awake, like the wolves fearing that surrendering control would create my death. Death was my loss
of control. Without my control I was sure I would lose everything, including myself. Tossing and turning in bed, I would
attempt to look at every angle and obsess frantically about the
potential harm of each option. Never did I believe that any
significant person in my life would be capable of holding up
the relationship. I *always* believed that I held the key to maintaining *our* relationship and the destiny we deserved. I consistently abandoned myself as I created a powerless situation
for both of us.

No one grows in these co-dependent situations. Dependency is created in the darkenss of fear. Obsession turned my
mind and heart back to my home of origin. I would constantly
drive myself insane worrying about what awful things would
occur if I didn't handle the situation correctly. I feared the
blame and shame that might transpire. I felt so small, almost
like I was six years old. I felt powerless and incapable, scared
and vulnerable. I fear what you fear: rejection, pain, and shame
if I do not "do it all."

## SUGGESTION:
## "Goodbye" Letter

Letter writing is a good tool to use to dissolve obsessive
behaviors. I have found it quite useful to write a "goodbye"
letter to the people or things I obsess around. For example, I
tell them I am no longer willing to obsess about them; that I
am no longer willing to hold them up; and that I am not
going to hold my life back any longer.

## SUGGESTION:
## Changing The Focus

Victims see events happening *to* them. Victimhood implies loss of control, in which you are powerless. When you
obsess, you become a victim. Obsession implies that your
focus is outside yourself and that you are internally defenseless to the stimulus.

Use the letters of the word **VICTIM** as an acronym to remind you of a tool in your recovery. Healing occurs when you change your focus from a victim to a **V**ery **I**ntimate **C**onnection **T**o **I**nternal **M**e.

This analogy will make you aware that obsessing creates a situation in which you look outside yourself for validation. Try looking inside.

## SUGGESTION:
## Slowing Down

Obsessing is the one thing over-responsible people do *perfectly!* If you fear you will be rejected, abandoned, disliked or discarded, you try to do and be everything to everyone. Sometimes you feel like the little Dutch boy who tries to plug up the hole in the dike with his finger, knowing it is humanly impossible to hold back the impending flood.

When you are obsessing, your mind racing out of control, try the following techniques to slow down:

1. Positive affirmations.
2. Journaling.
3. Verbally processing in a tape recorder.
4. Processing out loud with a friend.
5. Drawing a picture of your feelings with your opposite hand.
6. Exercising and then writing.
7. Calling your sponsor.
8. Writing out your feelings, *then* list things logically, after the emotions have all been validated.
9. Saying the serenity prayer.
10. Meditating.
11. Intervening and saying you will deal with the problem in an hour.
12. Surrendering and accepting that you can trust yourself to handle the situation.
13. Going to a Twelve-Step meeting.
14. Seeing your therapist.

15. Accepting that your life is unmanageable and turn it over to your Higher Power.
16. Taking a time-out from the situation.

Use caution and realize that it is important not to use over-spending, overeating, compulsive addictive relationships or any other addiction as a means of dealing with an obsession.

*Today I am becoming more patient
with myself as I change my behaviors.
I am trusting my ability to handle
situations as they arise in my life.
I am a beloved child of the universe.
I am enough.*

# Do You Have Difficulty Saying No And Establishing Personal Boundaries?

Pinnochio was shocked when he became liberated from his strings. He could move his limbs, which had been locked in his wooden body. The most bewildering aspect for the former puppet was his new humanness, which forced him to deal with his feelings. Wooden puppets, of course, feel nothing. They need not hurt, cry or feel anguish and shame when they do not care for themselves.

Self-abandonment was a difficult lesson for the vulnerable Pinnochio. The Blue Fairy had reminded him over and over again, "Remember Pinnochio, be a good boy, and let your conscience be your guide." Despite her warnings and those of a talking cricket named Jiminy, Pinnochio repeatedly ignored his inner voice. Eager to face life, Pinnochio was looking forward to attending school like a real boy. But he was stopped in process by two schemers who convinced the innocent boy that life would be easier in the theater. Unfortunately turning back temptation was not an element that Pinnochio had yet mastered. He quickly abandoned his conscience and fell prey to the dastardly duo. Without the ability to trust his inner voice, the wooden puppet ignored his need to say no and establish boundaries that would protect him from potential harm. This powerful lesson almost cost him his very *human* life!

Just like Pinnochio we often ignore our inner voice and listen to those around us. Without boundaries we grow more and more out of touch with our humanness. Pinocchio's self-abandonment created a long expanding nose that showed the world an obvious consequence of his self-abandonment. We too have markers that warn us that we are not establishing or maintaining our boundaries: Our body shouts out in physical pain — backaches, stomach aches, headaches, stress — but we repeatedly ignore the signs.

Recovery is learning how to connect with our inner self. Listening to our Higher Power is the way we establish our boundaries. Without that inner guidance system, we fall prey to our over-responsible destructive nature. When we are out of touch with our inner voice, we seek outward validation and approval to fill our inner void.

Jim was concerned about his girlfriend Beth, and her inability to have some quality time alone for herself. She seemed desperately in need of some time away from her house and children. Jim thought that volunteering to babysit might be an honorable and helpful means of allowing Beth to relax. Beth looked forward to those times of freedom he offered. Elated with her newfound rejuvenation, she began to ask Jim for more and more occasions so she might run errands and spend time with her friends. Jim, unable to set boundaries, began to submit to all of Beth's requests. Caught up in over-responsibility and the shame of feeling selfish or not enough, he abandoned his own commitments whenever Beth asked him for time for her needs.

Jim gradually realized that he was assisting Beth with her mental health but neglecting his own. Entrapped in his own web of caretaking, he found himself breaking plans with his friends and finding that now *he* had no free time. In rescuing Beth he had become a victim of his own caretaking behaviors.

Jim learned in therapy that the key is to find a balance between caretaking others and self-caring. Each one of us must develop and establish a comfortable, self-responsible balance point between the extremes.

Susan, a loving and caring member of Jim's group, said she had seen herself in Jim's story. She told the group she wore many different hats to accommodate different people in her life. If someone needed a mother, she was a sensitive caring mother. If someone needed a lover, she became a lover. She would determine which character each person needed, then go running to the hat rack and pick off the hat that gave her the appropriate appearance. As Susan looked around the group tears came to her eyes. "I haven't figured out which hat is mine. They are there for other people. I don't have any idea who *I am* because I'm always being over-responsible for others. Throughout my entire life I have rescued everyone but me."

We repeat and repeat and repeat the same dysfunctional actions over and over again because habits are hard to break. Breaking the pattern of caretaking is difficult. We developed these destructive habits over 20, 30, 40 or 50 years of continuous practice. We can't possibly expect to recover in a few weeks or months! Be patient with yourself.

## SUGGESTION:
## Pluses and Minuses

Each of your behaviors has positive and negative consequences. If there were no payoff for a specific act, you would not keep doing it. However, just because an action has a positive payoff, it does not mean that there are no negative effects.

For example, as a caretaker you receive approval and appreciation for your over-responsible behavior, but many times you overextend yourself. You may lose yourself in a relationship and victimize yourself. As you do everything for your focus person, you lose the ability to be responsible for yourself. It is important to realize that there are reasons for doing things as you do, even if the benefits are short term. For example, behaving in an over-responsible fashion may minimize your feelings of insanity, loss of control or guilt and maximize your feeling of approval.

It is important to realize that your behavior has been habitual over the years. A step forward in recovery is becoming aware of the positive and negative consequences so you can begin to change those habits and make new choices.

On the following worksheet (Figure 2), brainstorm the pluses and minuses of being the victim and the rescuer.

| | VICTIM | RESCUER |
|---|---|---|
| | | |
| Pluses: | 1.<br>2.<br>3. | 1.<br>2.<br>3. |
| Minuses: | 1.<br>2.<br>3. | 1.<br>2.<br>3. |

**Figure 2. Victim Or Rescuer?**

## SUGGESTION:
## New Options

Susan looked at the group in utter despair. "I'm just like one of those elephants in the circus. Have you ever watched one of those animals? A gigantic elephant tied to a little skinny stake in the ground spends its entire life walking around in a restricted circle. He is imprisoned by a tiny rope holding him captive like a prisoner in a world of noncaring humans. This powerful animal has been tied up for so long, he automatically knows just how far the rope will extend. His personal boundaries have been established through repetition, and he never tests the situation or implements a change.

"I was there once when they untied the elephant, and I couldn't believe it — he just stayed in the same circle of space! He didn't move outside that arena of imprisonment. He was free to make choices and leave the space he always knew, but he just kept going in the same circle. Oh my God — I realized, I've been doing the same thing!"

Susan realized she had imprisoned herself with the habitual responses to stimulus in her life. Despite the fact that she had viable options, she never *realized* she had them. Many of us have never taken the risk to claim our power and move outside our known responses. Over and over again we find ourselves doing the same things and experiencing the same consequences. We sometimes don't even consider that we have the freedom to make new choices and so we are blinded by our old behaviors. Like the elephant, we are caught in a tiny circle of insanity.

How many times have you told yourself you would never again be so over-responsible for others in your life? How often have you told yourself you would allow others the opportunity to learn to be responsible for themselves? When was the last time you stretched outside your narrow vision to see new options for yourself? You have locked yourself into a narrow vision of your world. Darkness must be illuminated by awareness before you can be guided by Light. To begin the process of change we must first *see!* Look around

— try stepping, one step at a time, out of your circle of over-responsible behavior.

## SUGGESTION:
## Bill Of Rights

The power of designing your own statement of rights is an empowering experience. These rights then become affirmations which are positive statements that can create a positive change in your life. You may never have learned to set boundaries, or learned how to say no, but you do have these rights. Establish your own guidelines, by writing your personal Bill of Rights.

Some examples might include:

- I have the right to say no!
- I have the right to a life without physical abuse.
- I have a right to live a life free of addictions.
- I have a right to change my strategy.
- I have a right to all my feelings.

- Take some time to write 10 (or more) rights for yourself:
  1. _____
  2. _____
  3. _____
  4. _____
  5. _____
  6. _____
  7. _____
  8. _____
  9. _____
  10. _____

- Try saying your rights aloud three times and feel the power. Witness it feels more empowering writing your rights.

- Many people have found it useful to state their rights in front of a mirror to experience the connection of the statement being mirrored back.

*As I venture into my recovery
I affirm my need to care for myself.
I am willing to allow others to be
responsible for themselves. The lessons
in my life are self-directed. I am
a beloved child of the universe.
I am enough.*

# 5

# Do You Lose Yourself In Yourself In Relationships?

She called him "Master" and dedicated her whole life to fulfilling his every wish. Always ready to please, Jeannie was willing to involve herself in any situation in an attempt to care for the handsome Colonel Nelson. In the TV show, *I Dream Of Jeannie,* she lived in a small bottle (she didn't deserve much space or attention) and was constantly obsessed with thoughts of pleasing her man. Jeannie was always so busy with her addictive over-responsibility that she had no real identity. In an attempt to gain Nelson's love and attention, she would literally change to become whatever she believed he desired. Jeannie was filled with shame because she never successfully accomplished her goal and was constantly pushing herself to do anything for his approval. Many times she would scream in frustration. But to her dismay her magical powers only altered his environment, not his heart. She created an easier life for him, but even her genie powers could not make her "enough." Nothing she tried *made* Colonel Nelson fall in love with her.

Over and over again I repeated the same destructive pattern with relationships in my life. I always gave everything, emotionally and physically, to others until I was painfully drained of my inner strength. Despite that awareness, my over-responsible behavior in relationships still brought the same painful consequences. Each time I hoped it would be different, but the lessons that I had learned in past destructive relationships had once again been lost along the path.

This repeated pattern of agony pierced my bleeding heart with a scalpel's precision. I had once again duplicated my past by holding everyone else up at my own expense. It felt so natural. It felt so familiar . . . and so necessary. All of my life I had been told it was "right" to help others who needed assistance. What else could I do in relationships with friends and lovers who meant so much? How else could I show caring and concern for the important people in my life?

I had difficulty discovering and defining the boundaries of where others stopped and I began. I felt like a giant well filled with cool crystal-clear water allowing each new traveler in my life to enter the hallowed ground of my magnificent watering place. Each one had his or her own desperate reason for needing the water from the reservoir. How could I say no to people in such dire need of life-supporting nourishment?

Slowly and predictably I gave away all of the power and inner strength I possessed in an attempt to make someone else's life more fulfilling and balanced. But, as I sustained *their* lives, I did not replenish my own diminishing reservoir of inner strength. I had never allowed myself the luxury of giving to myself when someone else appeared to need what I possessed. Sadly I had no real concept of what it actually meant to care for myself emotionally.

Focusing on others was always a means of gaining worth, approval and self-esteem. I was reinforced in the belief that I could create my self-esteem and self-worth by giving to and loving others. There was a payoff for always feeling so needed: I found myself bursting with energy as I watched needy recipients rejuvenate with my encouragement and support. Of course I mistakenly believed that the significant people in my life would reciprocate and would be just as giving if I needed *their* assistance. My gift was not unconditional; it incorporated the expectations of reciprocity.

But my inner reservoir was slowly being depleted and no one appeared to care, not even myself. I ignored all the telltale signs of the repeated pattern of destruction. My body screamed loudly to be treated with caution, as I minimized its cries. I dismissed the aches and pains in my lower back, which were trying to show me that I lacked support. I fueled my physical exhaustion with caffeine to produce constant output and stuffed my fears and anxiety with food. I was running on empty. Hitting bottom I realized that shame must be this pain deep inside . . . a pain only *I alone* could fill with loving myself.

Mark changed himself like a chameleon for every woman who walked into his life. An ugly, repulsive monster in his own eyes, he believed he was not capable and deserving of a relationship. Filled with anguish and self-hatred, and believing no one would love him for what he was, he decided that he must alter himself to be exactly what others desired.

Mark found himself in love with Laura. Totally lost to himself, Mark believed he was responsible for fulfilling all of Laura's desires and fantasies. If Laura wanted him to dress in grey, listen to jazz and give up his career, he followed her lead. Mark, a talented artist and writer, almost quit his job with a well-respected art company to comply with Laura's desires.

Sylvia wanted him to grow a beard, listen to classical music, and care for her every need. Once again, Mark did as requested and promptly disposed of hundreds of old rock 'n' roll records that he dearly loved and cherished. Just like a programmable computer, women entered information into Mark's memory banks and he matched the request to the appropriate response. Mark molded and contorted his body and mind to fit each person's fantasy. Hoping that these changes would make it "right" or "enough," Mark shut himself off from his true identity.

Doomed to his own sentence of terminal isolation and pain, Mark had a preconceived notion that it was his destiny to be alone because he could "never get it quite right with women."

"No matter what I do or how I change, I just can't find anyone to love me!" he said. Mark's eyes held the real truth: his inner identity had been lost along the way. The ugly monster that was repulsive to himself was actually the inner wounded child that he had molded and twisted to become what others desired. Empty and hollow, Mark had become everything for everyone and nothing to himself!

Short-term therapy centered around Mark's awareness of his own needs, wants and desires, as well as his pattern of over-responsibility and destructive self-abuse. Mark's first therapeutic assignment was to write a love letter to himself. Aghast, he decided that this was a ludicrous hoax disguised as therapy.

"Surely my therapist must have gone over the deep end! Doesn't she know that I don't have any love for myself? How can someone who hates himself so much write about any type of self-love? How can someone who sees himself as a monster write a love letter to his inner child?"

Despite his frustration with the assignment, Mark conceded and wrote what had been stuffed for so very long within his heart. The following letter is Mark's gift to himself. He looked deep within and found what was inside:

Dear Mark,

I know we haven't kept in touch very often, and I know you've been sad about that because I have been sad too. I'd like to take a step toward reconciling myself to you by thanking you for some things I've not given you credit for.

Thank you for not letting go. I've pushed you away, contorted you out of all recognition, many times hated you and sometimes wished you were dead. I blamed you for being weak, but you were strong enough to hold on even when the pain became so great.

Thank you for seeking counseling when you realized you couldn't make it alone. I accused you of living in a fantasy world, but admitting you needed help showed a real grasp of reality.

Thank you for not losing your trusting heart, which you exhibited again by sharing your journal with Joy. I thought you were a coward, but this showed courage.

I accused you of being a social misfit and a monster in the eyes of women, but you have proven me wrong.

Thank you for making me happy with your guitar. Your music releases me and often caresses me with the love and care you give each note.

Thank you for all the wonderful meals you've fixed for me, even though many might think them too extravagant for just myself. You found me worthy.

Thank you for being open-minded to new ideas, experiences and ways of thinking, and for breaking the pattern of narrow-minded prejudice passed along by your family.

Finally, thank you for your Spirit, which is the key to your own salvation. If allowed to fly free, it will carry you to the place you want and should be.

Be patient as I learn to love you.

Mark

## SUGGESTION:
## Love Letter To Yourself

Now it is time for you to unlock what you hold deep within yourself. I know that this is a scary risk for you to take. It is time for you to write a love letter to yourself. *There is no better time in the world!* You are *worthy* enough to give this gift to yourself.

I have given this assignment to thousands of clients and workshop participants, and have watched their amazement as they connected with their hidden inner children. As they wrote this letter to the part of them that had been locked so very deep within, they healed their wounded hearts.

Six months later I wrote a love letter to myself, and I share that love letter with you in this book's acknowledgments as part of my personal recovery. Writing this letter was very uncomfortable for me. I feared facing my inner child, but a miracle of self-caring and self-loving poured through my pen. I also feared that I was self-centered if I dared to even consider writing a love letter to myself. The gift I gave to myself was worth facing my fears.

The power of writing this letter can be quite liberating. Thousands of people around the country have told me this is one of the most valuable tools they have used to connect with their inner child. Many have told me how this process unlocked the door to the trauma, abuse, shame and pain that had been locked away from their conscious awareness. This tool in their recovery opened the door to further understanding, self-loving, acceptance and serenity.

Write this love letter to yourself with *your less-able hand.* If you are right-handed, use your left hand, if you are left-handed, use your right hand. Writing in this non-automatic fashion connects you to your inner child. Writing with your less-able hand means you automatically slow down your thoughts.

Use the space below to give yourself a miraculous gift.

Dear _____,

_____

_____

_____

_____

_____

_____

_____

_____

_____

_____

_____

_____

*I am worthy and becoming
self-nurturing toward myself.
I am making changes to re-parent
my wounded child. I am a beloved
child of the universe. I am enough.*

# Do You Find That You Often Do Not Live Up To Your Own Expectations And Goals?

Doomed to endless ridicule, poor Dumbo was the laughing stock of the "Biggest Little Show on Earth." At first glance all of the other elephants remarked that Dumbo was an adorable blue-eyed baby. "Better than I expected," whispered one member of the pachyderm contingency. "He is so adorable," remarked another proud friend of Mrs. Jumbo. But then it happened. The little baby sneezed and those enormous ears, almost as large as the baby itself, flopped out of the baby blanket! Jumbo Junior was dubbed "Dumbo" because he was a misfit in the elephant kingdom.

Condemned by all who saw him, Dumbo was sentenced to exile by the other elephants. He didn't live up to expectations and endured the constant shame that he was a "freak" and not worthy to himself or others.

"But I have so far to go. I'm sick of it all! It doesn't feel like I'll ever make it to my goals in recovery. I must stop this excruciating pain!" Debbie was disappointed with her perceived imperfect progress (based on unrealistic expectations of herself.) She looked toward the floor, like a rejected child who had just been scolded. "I've been in therapy for eight months and I'm still caretaking people in my life. When will I stop the pain and insanity and become totally responsible just for myself?"

Debbie was focusing her recovery on distorted thinking patterns that were self-critical and judgmental. These distortions had always reinforced her low self-esteem and kept her locked in constant mind racing and chaos. Debbie would sob uncontrollably in session and relate the story of her *negative wizards,* who were the people in her life who created pain and suffering. Only when she faced her real truth was she able to discover that *she* was her own negative wizard. Debbie had always allowed others the privilege of walking around in her head while wearing dirty shoes! She gave her power away and allowed the wizards to take command of her life.

Over-responsibility keeps us out of touch with ourselves and locks us in "dis-ease" with our thoughts and feelings. When we are over-responsible in our behavior, we *must* focus outside ourselves for approval and validation.

Debbie believed there was a magical destination in her recovery and personal growth. The magical moment for Debbie was "some place in time" when she would "do her recovery *perfectly*" and be totally responsible for herself and only herself. She cast these unrealistic expectations in black-and-white terms — either/or, yes/no, good/bad. By seeing things in such a perfectionistic way, she consistently maintained her "dis-ease" with her own growth.

Many of us see recovery as if we were a chocolate cake baking in a giant oven. We believe that after a certain amount of time we will be done cooking — that is, healed. We don't realize that the process of cooking *is* the celebration . . . the aroma of the cake is the serenity . . . the cake rising is the dawning of our enlightenment. Each moment and every baby step forward provides opportunities to witness new feelings, and the opportunity to rejoice in our progress and changes in our destructive patterns.

One way to alter unrealistic expectations and goals is to become aware of errors in thinking that keep us locked in shame and over-responsible patterns. The following informa tion will describe some errors in thinking and elicit some suggestions for insight and change.

Louise Hay teaches us that we can control our thoughts and create our lives to be as we desire. An essential element in recovery is understanding the "dis-ease" in our thought processes. We establish the meaning and direction of our future with our thoughts, and we give our thoughts power from past experiences.

For example, if we believe that all men are untrustworthy, then we will not be able to find any men that we can trust. We attain what we create. This attitude may have been developed based upon limited information in which one man in our early childhood was not trustworthy. Our early trauma established the mental generalization that *all* men were untrustworthy. When we become aware of the pattern, we gain the awareness needed for change.

One of the best sources of reference for understanding our distorted thinking is a list compiled by Jaffe and Scott in their book, *From Burnout To Balance*. The following "errors in thinking" illustrate how we make illogical conclusions in our thoughts and proliferate our co-dependent false selves:

1. All-or-nothing thinking
2. Overgeneralization
3. Mental filtering
4. Disqualification of the positive
5. Jumping to conclusions
6. Magnification (catastrophizing or minimizing)
7. Emotional reasoning
8. "Should" statements
9. Labeling
10. Personalization

## All-Or-Nothing Thinking

For many of us things are always at one extreme or the complete opposite. When we first discovered that we were caretakers and over-responsible for everyone in our life, we believed that the *only solution* for healing was to pull away totally from the people we have been enabling. Our all-or-nothing thinking can be compared to living in the Amazon for 25 years and deciding to move to the Antarctic for a climate change — a bit extreme!

## SUGGESTION:
## All-Or-Nothing Thinking

As you proceed in your recovery, notice the options that are now open to you. It is amazing how far you have come. Be patient with yourself. Your unrealistic expectations typically keep you moving down the tunnel at uncontrollable speed. Witness feelings, reward changes and listen to your inner child and Higher Power. As you proceed along this path you will witness it becoming more balanced and centered. With time and a trial-and-error process, you will find serenity and tranquility. Failure only comes when you do not risk at all.

How have you commonly used all-or-nothing thinking in your life? _____

_____

_____

## Overgeneralization

Dodie felt like her heart was breaking in two. "I know that he will abandon me. I have given all I have to Steven but it's *never* enough. No, *I'm never enough.* I couldn't love anyone any more than I do him. Why can't he just marry me? I know he loves me! What can I change about myself to make it better? What haven't I tried or done? He says he needs time, but I don't have forever. I want him . . . I need him . . ."

Dodie had listened to Steven's statements during the last month but overgeneralized his meaning. What Steven had actually told Dodie was that he loved her dearly and needed a little time to finish a project for his thesis. Dodie distorted his words (and their meaning) and created a situation that altered his viewpoint of "some time" into a definition that meant "forever." (ACoAs are constantly reading between the lines to be sure we don't get hurt or abandoned. By expecting the worst, we believe that we will be able to soften the blow by having "prepared in advance." In reality we have set ourselves up to experience unnecessary anxiety, since the dreaded worst case scenario rarely occurs). The fear that hides in our wounded inner child creates havoc inside us.

## SUGGESTION:
## Overgeneralization

How have you overgeneralized a situation in the last 48 hours? _____

_____

_____

_____

# Mental Filtering

How often have you taken in information through one viewpoint, as if everything was being sieved through a giant strainer made of all your past experiences and baggage? Our earliest modeling taught us to view life in our own "form" of reality. If we believe that all people are untrustworthy, we will find only untrustworthy people in our lives. Our mental filtering system creates our Truths.

Cari believed that *most* mothers abused their innocent little children. She was beaten, as were all of her sisters. She refused to have children because she feared that she would abuse them. The products of erroneous filtering created thoughts of helplessness and powerlessness in Cari's ability to parent children.

## SUGGESTION:
### Filtering

I generally filter my messages through the belief system that says: _____

_____

_____

_____

# Disqualification Of The Positive

Throughout his recovery Steven was seeing only his negative behaviors and actions. His self-judging and critical nature allowed him to discount any possibility of self-loving and encouragement. He always found one more thing that proved he was "not enough" to be viewed as a "a worthwhile person." This self-rejection was more devastating than any criticisms that could be uttered by others in his life. *He* was his own worst enemy.

"The only rejection that has any power is self-rejection." *(Emmanuel's Book* by Rodegast and Stanton). We have constantly been our most critical enemy. Isn't it amazing that we see everyone else as competent and positive except ourselves?

## SUGGESTION:
### Inner Strength

How often have you overlooked and minimized your inner strength? This error in thinking locks you in low self-esteem, approval-seeking, over-responsibility and fear. Look within and find the strength you hold. Discover your own empowerment. Acknowledge the positives!

What strength have you overlooked that is a positive aspect of your wonderment? _____

_____

_____

_____

## Magnification Or Minimization

Betsy's distorted thinking magnified all possible dangers in her daily life: "I always blow everything out of proportion. If something happens, I'll do all possible scenarios of the consequences in my head. I then create the worst imaginable scene to prepare myself for any occurrence. I feel safe using this protection because *no one* can hurt me as badly as what I have imagined. I protect myself emotionally by looking at all of the options to minimize my fear of the unknown. It's my means of controlling my fate. I feel in control if I cover all the bases so that I can determine my destiny."

Susan uses the opposite coping mechanisim, avoidance and minimization: She denies all thoughts and feelings about any circumstance in her life — the ultimate shutting down mechanism.

Susan and Betsy use different methods but both require distorted thinking, which keeps us from our real truth and feelings. When we magnify or minimize reality, we do not allow ourselves the opportunity to live in the present, the "now." When we live in the now, we learn to trust our inner voice. Since that voice speaks in gentle, soothing tones we must train ourselves to ignore the harsh accusing clamor of our critical voice inside.

### SUGGESTION:
### Magnify Or Minimize?

Which process do you typically use, magnification or minimization? How does it manifest? _____

_____

_____

# Jumping To Conclusions

I was taught to be hypervigilant as well as hypersensitive to outside stimuli. Years of experience taught me to live my life in accordance with outside forces. I was a responsible person, and being responsible meant action — quick and decisive action! I always made decisions based on limited information, however, because I never allowed myself the time I needed to assess a situation and feel appropriately.

When I jump to conclusions, I do not allow myself the time I need to seek internally the acknowledgment of my beliefs and feelings and create experiences that are positive for my growth. It is imperative that I accept the fact that *I deserve* to take the time required for sound decision-making. Avenues of choice differ in their relative importance; but some decisions can lead to life-changing routes. I owe it to myself to gather as many facts as are accessible and take time to decide, avoiding the familiar urge to jump.

## SUGGESTION:
## Jumping To Conclusions

With which people or situations do you find yourself jumping to conclusions? _____

_____

_____

_____

# Emotional Reasoning

Lynne said, "I can rationalize anything in my life. I can make sense out of being over-responsible for everyone in my life. I stay in my head and don't even listen to my true feelings because I don't have the time or desire to look into my heart. I *must* be responsible for others' needs and feelings and put my own feelings on the back burner. I do "mental" emotional reasoning to make sense out of nonsense. When you live in a chaotic home, you learn to make your own sense of any bizarre occurrence. It's a survival mechanism that kept me alive and motivated me to live through the trauma of each day."

## SUGGESTION:
## Emotional Reasoning

How do you keep yourself out of touch with your true inner voice? _____

_____

_____

# Shoulds

Louise Hay believes that "should" is one of the most damaging words in our belief systems. Our "shoulds" keep us locked outside our own focus. When we live according to "shoulds," we are commanded to live for someone or something besides ourselves. "Shoulds" tell us that we are choiceless with no options or means of being responsible to our own beings. They keep us disconnected from our Higher Power and personal growth.

## SUGGESTION:
## "Should" Messages

If you look at "shoulds" as a means of dis-ease within your life, you give yourself permission to change them into "coulds." In *You Can Heal Your Life,* Louise Hay offers this exercise:

What are the "should" messages in your life?

_____

_____

Which "shoulds" do you want to change into "coulds?" Are there any "shoulds" you would like to remove from your belief system?

_____

_____

_____

# Labeling

How many times have you labeled yourself as dysfunctional or a caretaker? How many times have you used recovery terms as a negative, critical way to label yourself? Words are potentially valuable tools, but too often we beat ourselves up with our own language. Even if we display certain negative qualities associated with a specific label, we must also acknowledge the positive elements that make us unique and lovable. Too often we allow a critical inner voice the luxury of controlling our lives. Sometimes we invite pain and judgment to pull up a chair and sit at our kitchen table and feast on our emotions and mind! Why do we continually invite dysfunction and pain into our lives? Do we actually want this pain to dominate us or is it just that the pain is so familiar?

## SUGGESTION:
## Labeling

Be gentle in your recovery and nurture yourself with loving encouragement. Labels keep you locked into judgment and critical self-sabotage. How have you destructively used labeling to sabotage your recovery?

_____

_____

_____

# Personalization

Jerry was humiliated by his behavior. "It's my fault, I should have known not to call her tonight. I always do the wrong thing with Tara. I never get it right. I try to be considerate and show her I care, but she says I'm always smothering her. I feel like such a fool. I'm obsessed with making it work with her. Whenever something goes wrong in Tara's life, I think that I must be responsible for her pain and try to find a way to fix the situation. I know my behaviors stem from my home-of-origin modeling.

"Whenever something went wrong when I was a child, I knew it was *my* responsibility, as the eldest, to discover a solution to care for my mother. She encouraged me to be her parent. I believed that everything that occurred was a personalization of my actions!"

## SUGGESTION:
## Personalization

I typically take on others' problems or concerns by personalizing:

_____

_____

_____

Together we have explored how distorted thinking processes keep our lives in dis-ease. It is difficult to break many of our habitual destructive tendencies, but it is possible to witness unbelievable changes within ourselves when we choose to look inward. The point of power is to reorganize our patterns. With awareness we can choose to change our lives and learn to be responsible for them.

Look at where you have been and where you are going. Be aware that you are perfectly and completely where you need to be at this moment. As you begin to look at your recovery in the moment, you can celebrate with immediate gratification the progress you have made as you embrace your growth. It is imperative that you celebrate your journey each day as part of your daily routine. You must learn to *give to yourself* as you have given to everyone else in your life.

*Today I witness the changes*
*I am making in my thoughts.*
*I hold the power to create*
*a loving safe place as my home.*
*I am a beloved child of the universe.*
*I am enough.*

# Do You Feel Worthy Only When You Get The Approval Of Others?

The Land of Honalee was inhabited by a
magnificent magical dragon named Puff. One
bright sunny day little Jackie Paper befriended the
gigantic sea serpent. That was the beginning of a
remarkably long-term relationship. Together they
traveled around the world as Puff became
responsible for the lad's psychological growth. Puff
and Jackie gave each other love, support and
approval within their wondrous relationship. Puff
gave all that he had, devoting his days to the eager
boy's enlightenment. Their adventures brought
them closer as each partner felt a never-ending
love and approval.

But one night Jackie Paper stopped visiting
his dear friend. Puff was devastated by the
abandonment. Puff literally fell apart — his scales
"fell like rain" without the approval and love of
his protege, upon whom he had centered his life.
Without his friend Puff could not exist, and
slipped back into his cave filled with shame
and the excruciating pain of his loss.

Devoting ourselves to someone else allows us to feel needed, wanted, powerful, important, useful and lovable. Many of us learned in our home-of-origin that we would be praised for our investment in someone else. We manifest caretaking behaviors in the hope of attaining the approval and the strokes we desire.

Many thoughts become obsessions: Will we gain the approval of others? Will we always feel inadequate and lonely? Will we ever feel like we are enough? Will we gain acceptance from others and diminish the infinite emptiness deep within our very being?

"I'm caught, and I can't get out. I just want to die," said Cindy. "Wasn't I the one who was always there? Wasn't *I* the *only* one who never left? Wasn't I the one who never abandoned him? I knew abandonment and rejection was one of his fears, and I was careful to make him feel secure. What I never did say to him was that I needed to feel secure, too. How could he abandon me after I did so much? I ended up looking like the bad guy in this whole thing. How did that happen? He just pulled away in a fashion that I never expected — he pulled away emotionally and I was thinking he'd leave me physically!"

Cindy desperately wanted to take her recovery into her own hands. All of her life she had felt "that life had happened to her" — she had no control of her destiny.

In her home of origin Cindy was targeted as the family scapegoat. She was imprisoned in her agonizing pain and excruciating shame. She tried everything imaginable to show her parents that she was truly responsible, caring and a *good* child. But they never saw what she accomplished or how hard she tried. Her family was blind to her attempts and only saw that she was the "crazy one" in the family. Cindy remembers the pain that stabbed deep into her heart when her mother looked into her eyes and told her she was "insane and wished that she was dead." Her dad used to tell her that he "couldn't stand being in her company" but he would come to her bed at night and sexually molested her. The shame swirled inside the little girl who felt such emptiness.

Even today Cindy carries those words deep within and still feels like she is a wounded eight year old who is totally unlovable. How could she be so shameful in the eyes of her family? Internally Cindy developed a means of protecting herself with layers and layers of psychological armor that served to numb her pain. The enemies were the people who were "supposed to be the parents that loved and protected her." What had she done that was so horrible? How could a little girl be so bad? Cindy swore to herself that someday she would make them see that she really *was* a good little girl. She committed herself to proving her worthiness and honor to her parents.

Because Cindy was never given the approval that she sought so desperately within her family structure, she searched out other people. Everyone in Cindy's life served as a testing ground for her unresolved issues of worth and shame. Cindy had no limits or boundaries. She would attempt to prove herself in any way with friends in her life. Anything and everything was possible if it might create a situation in which others would love her. She never said no to anyone's requests, regardless of how far she was pressed beyond her limits.

Aaron was the ultimate romantic challenge for Cindy. He was so much like her father — in fact they strongly resembled one another. But Aaron was different in one vital aspect: He was a recovering addict and Cindy's father was still an active alcoholic. This time she knew the scenario was perfect for her to do it "right" in her adult life. She had all the elements needed to revive the injustice of the past and "set it right by creating the perfect future."

Cindy knew that *she* was the only woman who could truly love Aaron. She believed this was the perfect relationship for her to be the "responsible person," and she would give him everything that he so desperately needed. She would help him to feel love in a way that would transcend anything he'd experienced before. Committed to her goal, Cindy believed she was the one person who could repair him.

Cindy gave and gave until it hurt. She gave her absolute all, catering to his most minute whim, determined to prove herself lovable and trustworthy. She must convince herself that she *was enough*. But, alas, her focus was on gaining the affirmation of someone else instead of on seeking an inner journey to discover her own "enoughness." If Aaron loved her, then she was lovable. The power to make life-changing decisions was outside herself. She allowed everyone to walk around in her head and Cindy drew conclusions about her own worth and esteem depending upon whether they shuffled their feet right or left.

Cindy wanted control of her life. She wanted to control all of the shame that had been placed on top of her by the world. But she felt helpless and hopeless to define her own destiny for the future. So she tried to affect and control the outside elements of the situation, which she believed would change the deep inner shame. That is why most of us try to control others. We use control to gain what we need outside ourselves. We attempt to make it right by having the play end differently this time. As the playwright we contrive, conjure, create or script the perfect scenario and make ourselves the heroes. The only means to achieve this goal is to do everything and anything that might force the play to evolve in the way we desire — even, paradoxically, at our own expense.

## SUGGESTION:
## From Self-Sabotage To Self-Love

As a co-dependent you believe that your worth is derived from the input of people around you. When you caretake, become over-responsible or engage in any other self-sabotaging behavior, you focus your attention on others' approval. The sun rises and sets by someone else's opinion of you. In my last book, *Addictive Relationships: Reclaiming Your Boundaries*, I wrote of the 10 Demandments that would insure an addictive or destructive relationship with others in our lives:

# The 10 Demandments

*10 Rules To Live By To Insure Unhappiness In A Relationship*

1. Thou shalt make me happy.
2. Thou shalt not have any interests other than me.
3. Thou shalt know what I want and what I feel without me having to say.

4. Thou shalt return each one of my sacrifices with an equal or greater sacrifice.
5. Thou shalt shield me from anxiety, worry, hurt, or any pain.
6. Thou shalt give me my sense of self-worth and self-esteem.
7. Thou shalt be grateful for everything I do.
8. Thou shalt not be critical of me, show anger toward me or otherwise disapprove of anything I do.
9. Thou shalt be so caring and loving that I need never take risks or be vulnerable in any way.
10. Thou shalt love me with thy whole heart, thy whole soul and thy whole mind, even if I do not love myself.

*—Anonymous*

Now let's rewrite the list in a more positive way. By restating the sentence and replacing the pronoun "thou" with your name, you become the navigator of your own journey.

## The 10 Rules Of Self-Loving

*10 Rules To Insure Self-Loving, Self-Caring And Self-Acceptance*

1. I, _____, shall make myself happy.
2. I, _____, shall listen to my inner voice.
3. I, _____, shall ask myself what I want and what I feel.
4. I, _____, shall appreciate myself and be loving of myself.
5. I, _____, shall allow myself to feel all of my feelings.
6. I, _____, am becoming more aware of my self-worth and self-esteem.
7. I, _____, will thank myself for "me" every day.
8. I, _____, shall be more loving to myself. I do this by not being critical or judgmental of myself for the risks taken and changes I am making.
9. I, _____, am willing to take risks because I am self-caring and self-loving.

10. I, _____, am becoming more loving of myself with all my heart, soul and mind.

For so long you have clung to the illusion that your family, friends and significant others were the "thous" in your life. As you put your name in the blank spaces, *you* become the navigator of your unique journey.

## SUGGESTION:
## Reinforcing Self-Love

It is useful to repeat the previous 10 statements to yourself each and every day for one month. This practice is a means of reinforcing and insuring the process of your self-loving, self-consideration and self-appreciation. Try saying them out loud to give your words the power you deserve. Better yet, say each one to yourself as you look into the mirror or record them into a tape recorder and play them back to yourself during the day.

*I am willing to face my shame
and address the pain deep within.
I am no longer willing to allow
the fear of myself to stand watch
over my fate. I am making
changes in my life. I am a
beloved child of the universe.
I am enough.*

# 8

# Do You Have Difficulty Celebrating Your Successes Or Seeing Your Accomplishments?

Dorothy and her friends frantically rush to get to the Land of Oz, where they hope to find their power. They believe the sooner they finish their journey, the sooner they will gain their reward. They do not know that they will find the reward within themselves. The characters run so quickly down the Yellow Brick Road that they do not witness their growth along the way.

Awareness is within their grasp, but there is never a moment to celebrate each gigantic step toward the Emerald City. Pushing, always pushing, they continue along the road to find what was inside all along. The Tin Man had always been caring and kind. The Lion had always been brave in the face of danger. The Scarecrow had always had brilliant ideas. Dorothy had always had the ability to see the power and love she held within. The difficult journey might have been easier if only they had known to look and trust what was deep within.*

*\*Adapted from Joy Miller's and Marianne Ripper's, *Following The Yellow Brick Road* (Deerfield Beach, FL: Health Communications, 1987).*

The journey we share — to heal our compulsion from caretaking and over-responsibility — is devastating. We must learn to witness and celebrate our successes, no matter how small they may appear. A toddler learns to walk by taking many spills and wobbly steps on the way to her encouraging parent. Tentatively she stands, moving each foot cautiously and deliberately. Fear changes to confidence. Success is reinforced despite the time-consuming effort that is demanded.

Our recovery is exactly the same. We must take baby steps to move forward in our recovery. Many times we unconsciously sabotage our success by not witnessing our efforts. Many times we negate or minimize our progress when we do not affirm our ability to face our fear and take risks to break our destructive pattern. We criticize and judge ourselves relentlessly for not doing more. We expect much more from ourselves than we do from others, whom we nurture and motivate into taking actions of these types. It is time to be loving to ourselves.

## SUGGESTION:
## Celebration Progress Sheet

Today I celebrate the awareness that I discovered today:

_____

_____

_____

_____

This is a big change/risk in my life because typically I would have:

_____

_____

_____

_____

My feelings concerning my changes and awareness are:

_____

_____

_____

_____

I will celebrate my success in the following ways: (For example: taking myself for a walk, allowing myself to have time for myself, giving myself the freedom to play, having an ice cream cone, giving myself verbal praise, giving myself a hug and so on):

_____

_____

_____

_____

## SUGGESTION:
## Visualization In Meditation

Choose a time when you will not be disturbed. Close your eyes, relax and visualize the following:

Think of yourself as a small child. So vulnerable. So delicate. So precious. Take a moment to look into the eyes of your inner child. Your child needs your nurturing, your support, the warmth of your gentle acceptance. Walk slowly toward your small child. You are safe; be gentle with yourself as you progress toward yourself. Sit next to your child for a moment.

Listen to what you need from yourself. Be gentle and accepting of what you are capable of giving to this small one. Each new awareness brings you closer to your safe home within as you nurture each other. Take time to be with each other. It is safe to be together.

Witness how the child grows and flourishes with your tender acceptance. Celebrate this change together. Love your child as you have loved so many others that you have become responsible to for so very long. Your child has waited so long for your acceptance and nurturing. Be patient . . . listen . . . you know how to love your child. The answer is inside. Listen and trust your own voice.

## SUGGESTION:
## Abandon Critical Self-Judgment

The first step in changing your behavior is to change your personal awareness. Too many times people in recovery disregard witnessing and celebrating their progress and positive changes. They are so "negativized" that they only focus on what they "didn't do," how they "weren't enough," or how the step they took was not perfect. Many people think that self-criticism and judgment are a means of motivating themselves into change. But they are not.

You are skilled in supporting and encouraging others in *their* recovery, and you routinely facilitate and become *their* motivating force. Yet you subject yourself to different rules and guidelines. You are so critical of your own performance that you never rejoice in your own accomplishments. Your cycle of rescuing is continuously self-propagated because you only appear to feel good when you support others.

Learn now to feel the ecstasy of celebrating your *own* recovery. You will change your caretaking to caring when you cherish even the smallest progress and abandon your need for perfectionism and critical self-judgment. You can accomplish this goal with vigilant awareness, practice and loving embracing of yourself. The final key is to turn yourself over to your Higher Power and forgive yourself.

## SUGGESTION:
## Celebrate Your Successes

Celebrating your successes is an essential aspect in your daily recovery plan. This simple little chart helps you look at how you typically handle issues, changes and progress in your life. Writing allows you the opportunity to visualize where you were, where you are going, and how to get where you desire. The empty squares at the bottom of the page are for specific issues that are individualized concerns for you. Use the worksheet as a daily progress sheet, or to facilitate a weekly inventory of progress. Consider how amazing this tool would be in your recovery if you had accumulated one year of weekly progress notes to witness your progress. This is an excellent mechanism for celebrating your successes and growth!

| The Issues | How I Used To Deal With It | New Behavior | Progress |
|---|---|---|---|
| Loss/Grief | | | |
| Honesty With Self-Awareness | | | |
| Maintaining Or Ending Relationships | | | |
| Fear | | | |
| Blaming/ Criticism/ Victimhood | | | |
| Abandonment | | | |
| Caretaking/ Over-Responsibility | | | |
| Fun/ Relaxation Self-Consideration | | | |

| The Issues | How I Used To Deal With It | New Behavior | Progress |
|------------|---------------------------|--------------|----------|
| Commitment | | | |
| Anger/ Resentment | | | |
| Self- Responsibility/ Make Decisions Based On My Need | | | |
| Changes/Risks | | | |
| Expression Of Positive Feelings | | | |
| Establishing Boundaries | | | |
| Perfectionism | | | |
| Workaholism | | | |
| Overeating/ Eating Disorder | | | |
| | | | |
| | | | |

*The key to my future is celebrating
my successes in the moment. I am
willing to look at my life from
a vantage point of acceptance.
As I refocus on self-encouragement,
freedom from self-criticism and self-judgment,
I facilitate my inner healing. I am
a beloved child of the
universe. I am enough.*

# Do You Often Find Yourself Physically, Emotionally And Spiritually Tired?

Cinderella awoke each morning to the same grueling drudgery of endless over-responsibility. Her daily itinerary consisted of being responsible for her two ugly stepsisters, Anastasia and Drizella, as well as her cruel stepmother. She would carry in the water, cook, mend, clean, scrub and wash for her irresponsible family members. Each day brought her only emotional, physical and spiritual depletion.

One beautiful day, quite out of nowhere, a magical cloud of stardust appeared in the kitchen. In the midst of it was a round-faced little woman. Cinderella stared in amazement at the woman, who pronounced herself a fairy godmother and commanded Cinderella to discontinue her co-dependent over-responsible behaviors and quickly leave for the ball at the royal palace. Cinderella tried to resist the changes. But the fairy godmother demanded that she take action and look at her options. She *could* go to the ball and become responsible for her own life.

As Cinderella boldly cast away the bondage of co-dependency and caretaking, she discovered magically that she had the ability to attain her dreams. Granted, she did meet a gorgeous prince along the way . . . but what changed her destiny was discovering the strength and ability to care for her own wants, needs and desires. This alone freed her from compulsive over-responsibility and caretaking.

In the past I always put everyone else's needs first, which inevitably meant that I did things at my own expense. Perhaps I continued this destructive behavior because I never learned to nurture myself. I gave others what I desperately needed, in the hope that I would gain a return of such loving and caring from others in my life. Many times I felt like no one could see how fragile and weak I was in my endless caretaking. I felt tired and angry when others seemed to take my hard work for granted. But I kept pushing myself along, refusing to slow down for my needs. My body would attempt to warn me with screams of stress and tension but I ignored them. Driven to prove myself worthy and noble, I charged forward like a knight on his trusty horse. Everything was a battleground, a challenge to prove myself in everyone's eyes. If I slowed down, I would be a failure and would surely be rejected.

That fear drove me to a point of no return. Physically, emotionally and spiritually dead, I hit bottom and surrendered to my Higher Power. I realized I was powerless to change others in my life and focused on myself. The journey is long, the road is bumpy, but I still trudge forward along my path.

With every change there is risk and risk is usually accompanied by fear. David Viscott's powerful book, *Risking,* states,

> In every risk there is some unavoidable loss, something that has to be given up to move ahead. Nothing overwhelms a person like the expected discovery of a loss he has not seen before. Even if you can't define the specific loss, any potential loss affects you.

Fear keeps us locked in our own pain, anger, resentment and destructive *status quo.* We timidly create a world that has no open doors and no choices. All we see is what is familiar because it is known. Change feels alien and uncomfortable. We dread risk because we don't know what to expect as a result of altering our behavior or feelings. Recovery is filled with new risks at every turn. How many times have you faced one of your issues only to turn around to find another issue looking you straight in the eye? A frequently accepted philosophy claims that the universe only gives you what you can handle. I'm sure many of us have wished that the universe would slow down a bit and give us a rest! But with each new risk comes an opportunity to learn a new lesson and receive the refreshment of healing in recovery.

Unfortunately many of us begin to sabotage our recoveries because we are afraid to face the next lesson. We avoid changes because we fear pain, failure or the unknown. This avoidance only delays our learning process. Life is about risks, changes and growth. When we ignore these three realities out of a misguided attempt at self-preservation, we numbly exist as mere empty shells, only shadows of who we are meant to become.

Sometimes risk means letting go of the people, places or things that are focal points of our anger and resentment.

Ilene recognized that she was becoming more and more over-responsible with people in her life after the dissolution of a catering business she operated with her best friend. She seemed to have lost both the friend and the business. How could something like this happen to someone who "took care" and nurtured a relationship and a business venture? Unconsciously she was trying to prove herself lovable and capable by being overly kind and giving to everyone who supported her.

Afraid to face her pain and anger, she stored it deep within, misusing 12-Step concepts in an attempt to stay in control. For eleven months Ilene had only fleeting thoughts of her associate and anger seethed like a volcano.

Sometimes insight just walks through the door. Ilene's insight occurred while listening to a Louise Hay tape on letting go of anger with people in our past. Immediately Ilene thought of her friend and raged inside, "I'm not letting go of this anger. I am not ready to let go, Louise! Why . . . Why . . . am I not ready or willing to let go? Why did she see me as unworthy?"

Confused and irritated with herself, Ilene felt like a wounded little child. She recognized that her anger was the only connection she had with her old friend and business associate.

"I always try to fix a relationship and become the caretaker and responsible one. That means that I alone am responsible for repairing every situation. Face it, I can't have a relationship with her. I can't find a way to heal my pain or shame. The only way to keep involved and connected to her is to hold on to the anger. I have held on long enough to the anger!"

If nothing changes, nothing changes. Ilene was holding back her growth and holding up the relationship by retaining the anger. That day she released the anger and relinquished the relationship with her best friend. She didn't let go out of spite or bitterness but in the spirit of freedom. Now that the essential awareness had finally come, she was no longer willing to curtail her growth by avoiding the risk inherent in change. Ilene faced her fear, shame and anger and took the risk to go on with her life.

## SUGGESTION:
## Holding Up And Holding On

What have you been "holding up" in a hope of "holding on" to a relationship?

_____

_____

How has this "holding up" affected your psychological health?

_____

_____

How has this "holding up" affected your spiritual growth?

_____

_____

How can you release this over-responsible "holding up" relationship?

_____

_____

Write an "anger" letter to the person that you are "holding up." When you are finished, complete the exercise with a "goodbye" letter and re-establish the caring for your own recovery as a priority in your life.

## SUGGESTION:
## A "Releasing" Letter

Write a "releasing" letter to your inner child. Write about allowing that child to discard the burdens that he/she has been carrying. Write as many feelings as you possibly can concerning the burdens the child has been carrying. Some people have found it useful to draw a picture of what the inner child appears to look like with all the burdens in his/her life. On the back of the paper, for closure purposes, draw a picture of how the child would look free of the encumberments.

## SUGGESTION:
## Nurture Your Inner Child

As a child you had many ways to nurture yourself — a blanket or a stuffed animal, books or fantasy, imaginary friends or parents. As an only child I derived nurturing from my pet beagle, who was *always* there to love and console me in times of need.

What did you use in your childhood to nurture your inner child?

_____

_____

_____

_____

Which of the above can you integrate in your life today?

_____

_____

_____

_____

What other mechanisms could you consider as a means of nurturing?

_____

_____

_____

_____

## SUGGESTION:
## Motivate Yourself

You are proficient at caring for and motivating others in their recovery. You have an endless supply of options and new concepts that help others change their viewpoint about themselves.

What are some of the techniques that you use to motivate others to increase their self-esteem and self-worth?

_____

_____

_____

_____

How can you integrate some of the above tools into your own recovery and self-nurturing?

_____

_____

_____

_____

Take time to acknowledge your success in self-nurturing each day. Affirm your successes each night before you fall asleep.

*Today I will discover and affirm
my own self-nurturing. I am making
changes that change my life in
positive ways. I am a beloved
child of the universe.
I am enough.*

# 10

# Do You Have Difficulty Expressing Your True Needs, Wants Or Desires?

Scarlett O'Hara is filled with shame and sorrow.
She realizes that her valiant attempt to make
Ashley propose marriage is only a dream. She
stands, dazed and alone, in the midst of the
commotion caused by the declaration of the
South's admission into the Civil War. The cries of
excitement fill Twelve Oaks, but Scarlett is
immobilized by her own fear of abandonment.

From afar she hears the cries of Charles
Hamilton, who breaks her spell of despair. Caught
in the desperation of the moment, Charles
impulsively risks rejection and asks for Scarlett's
hand in marriage. Scarlett realizes that she can
gain revenge on Ashley and save face in the light
of terror. Despite her lack of love, caring or
interest in Charles, she accepts his proposal.
Scarlett knows she is going against every ounce
of sense within, but her fear of being alone cloaks
her reality. To prevent her heart from taking
charge, she quickly tells Charles that he must
ask her father's permission and blessing of the
wedding proposal at that very instant.

Many times, like Scarlett, we dismiss our needs, wants and
desires out of a destructive fear. This pattern of co-dependency
locks us in the despair of self-abandonment, while our over-
responsible caretaking voice negates our inner true voice.
Struggle as we may, too often we allow ourselves to destroy
our journey into recovery. Filled with shame, we never allow
ourselves the time and nurturing to quietly listen to our inner
voice. We put our needs and wants on the back shelf as we
dismiss the wounded child within.

Dawn lived in the terror of her own prison. Cut off from her
own needs, she lived her life vicariously through her daughters. She gave until it hurt, neglecting her own needs in an
attempt to have her daughters live differently than she had.

As Dawn progressed in therapy she realized the only means
of bettering her daughters' lives was by working on her own
recovery issues. She created a healthier world for herself as she
allowed her daughters the opportunity to grow responsibly.

## SUGGESTION:
## What Do You Value Or Need?

You may never have allowed yourself the time and energy
to establish a list of what you value or need. The following is
a brief list of some options you may desire. Use the list, and
search your heart for additional options to evaluate the questions that follow.

What do you value or need? Please circle the items which
hold a high value or priority in your life at this moment.

1. Being known as an authentic individual
2. Self-confidence, self-esteem and self-worth
3. Honesty
4. A meaningful relationship
5. Life with meaning and purpose
6. Physical appearance
7. Spiritual growth
8. Educational growth

9. Financial stability
10. Health
11. A good relationship with your Higher Power
12. Accomplishing worthwhile things
13. A secure family life
14. Open communication with others
15. A comfortable home
16. A stable job
17. Creativity/potential
18. Owning things of worth
19. Intimacy with another human being
20. Freedom to live as you desire
21. An opportunity to give to the world in a meaningful fashion
22. Self-actualization
23. Travel, recreation, fun
24. Meaningful friendships
25. The opportunity to take personal risks
26. The desire for excitement and challenge
27. The need for emotional independence
28. The need for time alone
29. The need for control
30. The need to receive nurturance from your mate
31. The need for mutual openness
32. The need to feel loved
33. The need for loyalty
34. The need for stability
35. The need to have sexual expression

What do you need or value in a love relationship?

_____

_____

_____

_____

_____

_____

_____

What do you need or value in a friendship?

_____

_____

_____

_____

_____

_____

_____

Now look at your list. How can you assist and nurture yourself in acquiring the things that mean so much to you? Sometimes it helps to ponder what you would do to assist others in your life if *they* desired the above items. Use this as a guide to self-nurturing.

How can I help myself get what I value? Use extra paper to set up a plan of action.

_____

_____

_____

_____

## SUGGESTION:
## What Holds You Back?

Happiness . . . can grow in any soil, live in any condition. It defies environment. It comes from *within;* it is the revelation of the depths of the inner life as light and heat proclaim the sun from which they radiate. Happiness consists not of having, but of being; not of possessing, but of enjoying it. It is the warm glow of the heart at peace with itself . . . Happiness is the soul's joy in the possession of the intangible . . . Happiness is paradoxical because it may coexist with total sorrow and poverty. It is the gladness of the heart, rising superior to all conditions . . .

— William George Jordan

Finding the happiness that you deserve and desire is an inner journey into the depths of your very soul. As you re-parent yourself, search the caverns of your being and heal the hurts of your inner child. You will discover that you need to be responsible for your own self as you heal your shame. No one else can heal you — you are your own slayer and your own savior. You only need to realize that you hold the power of your life in this very moment.

What has kept you from exploring yourself? What has held you back? If you look at your strengths, your needs, and your wants, what might you discover? Take a moment to think about the following:

What is the possible benefit of looking at my needs, wants, and personal strengths?

_____

_____

_____

_____

_____

What might be holding me back from taking responsibility for myself (my needs, my wants, and my strengths)?

_____

_____

_____

_____

_____

The following are examples of some insights you might discover:

*What is the possible benefit of looking at my needs, wants and strengths?*

1. Reinforcing myself/validation/affirmation
2. Increasing self-worth and self-esteem
3. Connecting with my inner child/self
4. Increasing confidence in myself and my abilities
5. Refocusing from negativity to a positive outlook of myself

6. Discovering that I can reparent myself
7. Discovering that I can be a positive self-motivator in my life
8. Discovering what I am capable of accomplishing
9. Establishing an awareness of my bill of rights
10. Realizing that I am "enough"

***What might be holding me back from taking responsibility for myself and my needs, wants and strengths?***

1. Expectations of myself
2. Fear of discovering that I am not "enough"
3. Fear that if things are too good, a disaster may be looming in the future
4. Fear of breaking the old home-of-origin modeling (over-responsibility, caretaking, enabling, approval seeking) and not knowing how to perform or be able to control the outcome

As we look within to find our answers, we discover it is always easier to look at what others wanted and needed instead of looking inside. We manifested our co-dependency by over-responsibility and caretaking, which is the enemy of our personal happiness. We were taught to ignore our own lives and focus on others in an attempt to fill our empty hole of worthiness. We were reinforced by so many to live life for others, not ourselves. We have become victims of our own making, often without realizing the self-destructive process was taking place.

Today we realize we are responsible for our own destinies. We cannot control others in an attempt to gain self-approval. The healing that we desire comes from inside, not from outside. **If we do not go within, we go without.**

*Today I am becoming more in touch
with my inner happiness. I am
discovering my strength and my power.
I believe that I am capable of reaching
the stars. I am a beloved
child of the universe.
I am enough.*

# 11

# Do You Feel As If No One Appreciates What You Do And Therefore Everyone Takes You For Granted?

Ricky Ricardo career was constantly on Lucy's mind. She was dedicated to furthering his success at the Copacabana, and was always scheming in an attempt to promote her husband's career. She was prepared to utilize any far-fetched stunt that might prove effective, and would even elicit the assistance of her obliging neighbors, Fred and Ethel Mertz.

Together the threesome became over-responsible for the seemingly weak band leader. Despite Lucy's efforts, Ricky never realized the extent of the caring and energy that Lucy expended to make him successful. Her actions, given from a place of love, usually made her appear to be a buffoon and her outrageous efforts in his interest humiliated and shamed her.

The show was called *I Love Lucy,* but we never witnessed anyone, especially Ricky, loving the real Lucy. (Did Lucy ever know the real Lucy?) What we saw was Ricky scolding, judging and criticizing Lucy for all of her stunts. Regardless of the fact that she was mobilizing the efforts in his behalf, Lucy was shamed for her endeavors. She was never appreciated, rewarded or given ample praise (or a part in the Copa show) for all of her escapades.

Lucy's over-responsibility for Ricky's success illustrated her immense co-dependency. Each scenario reinforced her belief that she was "not enough" to be approved, loved or nurtured.

Shakti Gawain states in *Living in the Light:*
    You can't be a rescuer unless you believe in and have a victim inside. It may appear, however, that some people are strictly rescuers or victims. Or at the extreme side, there are people who are always in a mess and desperately need the help of others. These are martyrs whose meaning in life depends on saving others. Usually we bounce back and forth between these roles in less extreme ways.

We lightheartedly say, "As adult children we don't have relationships, we take hostages." Author John Lee states the same philosophy in a different way: "We don't do relationships, we do projects." Many of us chuckle and giggle, but a thread of truth shakes our very core. This *is* "our Truth." Painfully we admit that we do take hostages by using caretaking, enabling, or over-responsible behaviors. We turn our focus outward in the hope of finding someone to fix.

Some of us assume the opposite role and we allow ourselves to be the hostage (the victim). We do the "dance of intimacy" in a painfully agonizing, repressive fashion, never quite feeling the power of our own responsibility. Consequently we live in shame. We never allow ourselves the opportunity to discover our true power; we are fearful and feel powerless against the outside forces determining our destinies.

Many times we are both victim and hostage-taker. For instance, as compulsive lovers we take a hostage and completely overpower and smother the focus person. At that exact moment we also become the victim of our own destruction and set up a life of pain, agonizing compulsion and obsession. We become both victims and rescuers, trapped in the co-dependency.

When we envision the role of the caretaker, many of us think of responsible first children. But each child, no matter what the familial role, has the *potential* to hold others up — and hold themselves back. Even the family scapegoat can be a caretaker.

Stan was filled with pain and shame. He knew he was the family scapegoat and hated that role. His family saw him as irresponsible while they saw his brothers as good and righteous. He was the child who was "just a little different" and rebellious. Alcoholism proved an easy escape from his familial pain. Drinking covered up his lack of confidence and helped him deal with the shame of "not being good enough" in comparison to his "saintly" brothers.

In therapy Stan began to realize the artificially induced power he derived from drinking, and struggled with home-of-origin issues to bravely face his addictive personality and chemical dependency. To his dismay, despite his sobriety and his dedicated recovery program, the way he was viewed in the family did not change. Hurt and confused, Stan reached his fourth year of sobriety and discovered he was still required to maintain the family scapegoat role. It didn't appear to matter to his family that he was sober, hard-working, industrious and integrating a strong recovery program.

Deep within Stan knew he *always* put himself on the line for those he loved. His caretaking was much different than that of the over-responsible first child, but his intentions to prove himself worthy and his wish for approval were the same as any caretaker, despite their familial role. Both Stan and the over-responsible first child have learned to do for others at their own expense. Both performed and continue to perform "their own magic" in an attempt to gain love and acceptance.

As the scapegoat Stan charged like a frenzied soldier through a deadly minefield to fight for the common good. (In fact Stan actually put himself on the line and enlisted in the army. He purposely asked for a dangerous assignment overseas in an attempt to gain the acceptance and patriotic accolades of his family.) Everyone around Stan learned that he would be the "savior" and make the "wrongs of the world right." His methods were usually a bit unorthodox and sometimes quite harsh, but he ran fearlessly into the heat of chaos to save his friends and those he loved.

As Stan saved the primary people in his life, however, he realized that they became more and more irresponsible and dependent on his caretaking. The more he saw them retreat and become helpless, the deeper he ran into the psychological minefield. Each time, Stan fought the hand-to-hand battle for what he believed was best for those he loved. The people around him seemed to take his courageous behavior for granted. "Something must be wrong with me," he cried, "I just can't seem to do enough for these people! I keep doing everything for my friends, and they give me less and less. I want to tell everyone to go to hell!" Through months of therapy Stan realized his destructive pattern of caretaking and discovered how he had lost himself (actually given himself away) through the years. When he learned that he must first take care of himself, he found the inner serenity he needed to integrate a 12-Step Alcoholics Anonymous program into his personal life.

Pam, another caretaker-scapegoat, explored her over-responsibility. "I'm a 'crusader' and my mission is proving that I can be good. I do things for others in the interest of truth and justice. I find that I must fight injustice and be a savior of those I love. Don't you see? It's the ultimate challenge." Pam explained that she had never "done it right" as the family scapegoat.

"Whatever the cost, the risks are basically nothing to me — I'm blinded by the goal of seeking out the truth. When I get in this caretaking phase, I see no available options. All I know is what I *have to do*." Pam discovered part of her compulsion was the excitement in the challenge of finding a way to prove herself noble to herself and the world. While she looked outside to find the means of fixing the inside, the *truth* she was seeking was hidden internally!

As I have grappled with turning my dream of recovery into reality, I have discovered it is not as simple as it looks to the outside world. I realize each of my smallest goals has hundreds of little steps and risks to undertake as I proceed down my path. It's no great surprise that I avoid risks and sidestep issues intermittently in my recovery! This "recovery thing" is *a lot of hard work!*

One way to face my new issues in recovery was to use a plan of attack to accomplish my goals. For instance, when I was four years old and wanted to ride a new red two-wheeler, I had to learn in small, specific steps. First of all there were precautions to protect my risk-taking into the scary world of the unknown. My parents made sure that I had training wheels on my new little bicycle and told me to wear long pants to avoid scraped knees from falls that would surely come. Next they gave me directions on how to get on this strange vehicle. Both scared and excited, I sat on the uncomfortable little seat and found myself wobbly, quite unsure of my fate. The bicycle tipped and tilted a bit, but my supportive parents held me on. I felt quite sure that my parents would protect me from all pain. Then they told me to pedal the bicycle. With nurturing voices they told me the direction to push my feet, and then told me that, at the *exact same second,* I had to concentrate on where I was going. Were they nuts? How could I possibly watch where I was going and also do this pedaling stuff?

With much practice and dedication, however, I got the idea of how to pedal and even figured out how to keep it going in a straight line. Just when I had mastered the whole concept, and to my utter disbelief, my parents told me to turn. "Turn?" I whispered. "I'll just always go straight ahead! I can't turn this without falling, so forget it! I'll just walk everywhere I want to go!"

With practice, and many scrapes and scratches, I learned to ride the two-wheeler. But things never stopped changing. Just when I got to the mastery level, the next conquest was to ride without the training wheels. Once again, just when you think you have figured out a change . . . *change changes.*

Reclaiming ourselves and facing over-responsibility and shame are very much like riding that new red two-wheeler.

But some of us unfortunately had no physically or emotionally available parents to teach us how to ride those bikes. Consequently we watched others carefully and tried to figure it out on our own. Petrified that our inability would confirm the inner belief that we might not "be enough" or "do it right," we just decided to improvise through all encounters of risk and change in our lives. In adulthood we have continued looking for the "manual" on every subject available to give the outward illusion that we are all-knowing and capable. We just want to look normal in the world that feels so foreign to us.

## SUGGESTION:
## Reclaiming Chart

Bonnie always took care of everyone in her life. She was the perfect junior therapist for her friends, responsible for the success and continuation of all relationships. In group therapy she believed her personal issues "were just not as important and relevant" as everyone else's. She minimized her own needs in an effort to care for others she saw as more needy.

Finally, however, she realized that enabling others minimized her own benefit from the therapy group process. Others within the group viewed her as superior, and "too healthy" to even be in the group. No one knew about her pain because she was too concerned about focusing on their pain, ignoring her own. Bonnie knew the intensity of her wounded heart which was locked deep within, but you can't be a junior therapist and also get involved in your own issues — not when you're an over-responsible caretaker for the entire world!

The following chart illustrates how Bonnie eventually sorted and reclaimed her inner strengths in her individual therapy sessions.

## Bonnie's Reclaiming Chart

*Issues to be addressed:* caretaking/over-responsibility for others.

### Consequences:

1. I do more work and feel like I'm always "doing it all" (physically and emotionally) for everyone in my life.
2. People become more dependent on me. Others have expectations of my behaviors, reactions and feelings.
3. I sabotage myself in my recovery growth process.
4. I ignore my wants, needs and desires.
5. I put myself last.
6. I overload myself and become overwhelmed physically and emotionally.

### Risk/Fear

1. Abandonment.
2. Not being needed (worthy).
3. Anger from others.
4. Fear that I will not be liked or accepted by others.

### Self-Talk

1. I'm not worthy.
2. I'm not enough.
3. No one appreciates me and I'm taken for granted unless I do everything.
4. If I produce, then I will be lovable and capable.

### Rules

1. I must always be aware of what others want.
2. I must always help someone in need.
3. I must always take care of people who need me.
4. I must meet everyone's expectations.
5. If someone needs me, I must help them immediately, no matter what is occurring in my life. Others come first.

### New Rules

1. I am becoming aware of my over-responsibility and its effects.

2. I am becoming aware of the positive changes in my behavior.
3. I am becoming inwardly loving and attempting to be less critical of myself.
4. I am becoming more attuned to my inner voice so I may hear my wants and needs.
5. I am becoming more considerate of what is best for my personal growth.
6. I am becoming more willing to allow others to be responsible for themselves.

## New Self-Talk

1. I am enough.
2. I will be aware of my needs, wants and desires.
3. I am worthy and lovable.
4. I am finding my strength within myself.
5. I am whole, I am complete, I am perfect just as I am today.

## What I Can Gain By Altering My Behavior

1. Healthier relationships with myself and others.
2. More balanced life (less ups and downs).
3. Better physical health.
4. Self-consideration.
5. Feeling more in tune with myself.
6. Decreased co-dependency.
7. Increased self-loving, self-nurturing and reparenting.

The following is a blank chart that can be photocopied for your own personal use.

# My Reclaiming Chart

### *Issue to be addressed:*

1.

### *Consequences:*

1.
2.
3.
4.
5.

### *Risk/Fear:*

1.
2.
3.
4.
5.

### *Self-Talk:*

1.
2.
3.
4.
5.

### *Rules:*

1.
2.
3.
4.
5.

## *New Rules*

1.
2.
3.
4.
5.

## *New Self-Talk*

1.
2.
3.
4.
5.

## *What I Can Gain (Alteration Of My Behavior)*

1.
2.
3.
4.
5.

*As I learn to care for myself, I expand in new ways. My serenity comes from knowing the difference in how I can create change. I am a beloved child of the universe. I am enough.*

# Were You The Family Caretaker In Your Home-Of-Origin? Do You See Yourself Now As A Fixer Or Caretaker?

Lady's life was devoted to caring for Jim Dear and Darling. Each day the cute blonde cocker spaniel puppy would bring them their mail and newspaper and receive a pat on the head. Lady knew she was *expected* to be responsible. It was her duty to be responsible for the security and protection of her family in all ways. This responsibility included policing the territory around their homestead and constantly being vigilant for any dangerous intruders near their home.

Lady would guard her family's safety with her very life. When the new little baby joined the household, the dog became even more passionate in her need to provide over-responsible protection for her beloved family.

Whatever the danger, Lady was prepared to face any and all situations that might endanger her loved ones. Her hypervigilant behavior reminds us of ourselves: We are constantly on guard, waiting for a crisis that we can fix and protect. Our role mandates that we are responsible for any decisions, as well as consequences incurred by those we love and protect. Certainly this over-responsible behavior demands that we stay on top of all situations and remain at the will of others. Whenever we focus outside ourselves, we abandon our own recovery.

Marian, an extremely sensitive first child of a drug-abusing mother, was always the responsible caretaker for her family. Many times Marian would be the responsible "parent" because her mother was incapable of functioning due to her prescription drug addiction. She was forced to play the role of the adult parent nurturing and supervising her two younger brothers, even though she was a mere child herself.

At the age of eight Marian was cooking, cleaning and caring for all the needs of her brothers, aged six and four. For her over-responsibility and loss of her own childhood. Marian was rewarded with the intermittent praise of her workaholic industrialist father: "You're such a help, Marian! What would I do without you? Your mother is so irresponsible and lazy. She and those drugs . . . they will be the death of us all. You're the only joy in my life." Marian lived for those reassuring compliments and hugs of appreciation from him, even though they came infrequently.

But the doom of addictive behavior lurked in the air. To Marian's confusion and dismay, her mother would shame and scold her for being lazy and not doing enough in the house. Despite Marian's increasing attempts to do more housework and care for her mother's needs, she was blamed for her mother's irrational behavior, which included traumatic suicide attempts.

On each occasion Marian would witness her mother's despair, characterized by sobbing episodes as she complained of being so overworked by "those three demanding, wild children." Marian would be scolded for her laziness and childish playing and dawdling. Didn't her mother see that she was doing the best she could? Didn't she see she was trying *so* hard to do it right?

As Marian grew up, she had her antennae out tuning into anyone else's needs. The possibility of assisting someone who *needed* her stirred feelings within Marian: the desire to help, need for approval, hypervigilant sensitivity. She feared that her actions might not be appreciated and rewarded with approval, but she knew she must act and be responsible. The shame of not acting was always greater than passivity on any issue. This fear was reinforced and cemented in that familiar, nagging message from her home-of-origin.

Once again her fear was that she would gain only contempt (old shame messages from her mother) and disapproval. Despite that fear Marian habitually played the same role, compelled to seek approval in an attempt to gain self-acceptance. She complied with everyone else's wishes with no regard to her own personal boundaries or needs. (In fact Marian had not discovered her boundaries or rights because she was not aware that she was entitled to such rights!)

Overwhelmed with responsibility and exhausted by the expectations of others, she nurtured her despair with food. Food was the *only* thing that was always there for her. In the beginning, her binge eating was a subconscious attempt to fill the empty pit of "not feeling enough." But the empty hole became more and more difficult to fill and required more and more anesthetizing food. Still the pain continued to surface and Marian found it more difficult to suppress her intense feelings. She felt like a zombie walking through life waiting for a jolt of electricity that came only when others showed approval of her behavior. Isolated from her own needs, she escaped deeper into her compulsive overeating to freeze her feelings.

## The Caretaking-Apathy Spectrum

Caught in caretaking and over-responsibility, we desperately struggle like insects caught in a spider's web. Having fallen prey to the tyrant that compels us to regard things only in black-and-white terms, we have learned to believe that we must either caretake others or be seen as the opposite — irresponsible and apathetic. Apathy and caretaking are two divergent extremes, destructive traps that keep us entangled in fear and pain. Each choice is an opposing end of a spectrum which appears to have no available options or choices (see Figure 3).

Apathy                                                              Caretaking

**Figure 3. The Apathy Caretaking Spectrum**

Far too many of us have experienced the feeling of insanity because of our over-responsibility and shame. Knowing only the extreme edges of chaos, we constantly race from caretaking to apathy when our buttons are pushed. We use each end of the spectrum as a defensive mechanism to save ourselves from pain. At these extremes body, mind and spirit are not congruent. This insanity keeps us blinded and trapped in our destructive behaviors and shame messages. As we explore the motivation of each extreme, we discover many similarities.

## Caretaking

These are the behaviors of caretaking:

1. We act in the interest of other people's needs, wants and desires.
2. We take on responsibility and risk ourselves for others in our lives.
3. We lose ourselves (needs, wants, desires) in the process. We focus on others so we have no motive to focus on our own pain and issues.
4. We act out of our need to control.
5. We act in the hope of gaining the approval and love of others.
6. We maintain emotional denial of our own issues because we are focusing on someone else.
7. We get caught in the rescuer-victim triangle. This triangle, described by Marsha Utain and Barbara Oliver in

their book, *Scream Louder,* illustrates how we rescue a victim and later become the victims of our own self-sabotage.

8. We keep our victims locked in the belief they are not enough and are incapable of caring for themselves. (Notice that the word caretaking has the root word "take" — take away others' power to grow.)

9. We discover that we live in the seemingly endless *blame* and *shame* cycle. Notice that both words contain *am.* The hidden message is, "I *am* nothing if I am not caretaking." What I *am* is determined by what I do and how I perform. If I do not perform in the "acceptable" fashion, then I will experience blame and shame.

10. We assess ourselves and others around us with critical and judgmental pronouncements.

11. We are constantly trying to "do it all" in an attempt to "do it right." In the quest for *ultimate* perfection, we discover that there is no possible way to cancel out our belief that we are "not enough" and although in reality we never can attain that elusive pinnacle of perfection, the striving for it remains relentless.

## Apathy

These are the behaviors of apathy:

1. We appear selfish and self-absorbed to other people in our lives.

2. We stay in denial because we numb ourselves to the outside world and its pain.

3. We appear irresponsible and indifferent.

4. Our uncaring attitude traps us in inner (self-awareness) and outer isolation (physical isolation with others).

5. We find we need to escape from the world and appear unresponsive. Our defense mechanism traps us in depression and hopelessness.

6. We believe we are not enough, which is the basis for our need to pull inside for protection.

7. We lose ourselves by numbing our feelings, wants and
desires and therefore are out of touch with ourselves.

8. We too are caught in the blame-and-shame cycle. We
continually blame ourselves for lack of self-esteem,
while others blame us for apparent uncaring behavior.

9. We become the victims of our own lack of action.

10. We are critical of ourselves and others.

11. Psychologically we feel invisible — empty and dead
inside. We don't show the real pain as we cry in our
own way for help, making it difficult for others to rec-
ognize there is a need to be met.

As we look at the extremes of both divergent traps, we
discover there can be movement (choices and options) toward
balance. Figure 4 shows the movement toward the middle of
the spectrum.

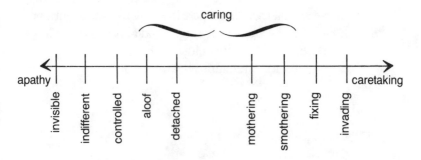

**Figure 4. The Caretaking-Apathy Spectrum Revised**

The spectrum has a center range (please note: this is a
range, not a specific spot or "perfect" resting place) that we
discover along our journey into recovery. The midrange between *apathy* and *caretaking* is *caring.* Caring has two essential elements: caring for others and caring for oneself. Each
component is required to maintain the health-recovery triangle
of body, mind and spirit (see Figure 5).

As we learn to move into the grey areas between the black
and white extremes, we discover that healthy caring allows

others to be self-responsible. It is very easy to be consumed by guilt and condemnation when we realize our enthusiasm to help others has actually constricted them.

**Figure 5. The Health-Recovery Triangle**

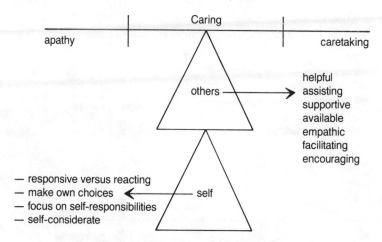

**Figure 6. The Apathy-Caretaking Spectrum
And Health Triangle**

As we free others to be self-responsible, we learn to become helpful, assisting, supportive, empathetic, facilitating and encouraging. This does not mean that we pull away totally from those we care about; rather we give expression to a loving means of "being there" without "doing it" for them. This healthy distancing allows us to be an active part of people's lives and to act as their mirror, reflecting back information to expedite their growth and allow them to integrate their recovery uniquely. A good therapist, for example, facilitates, assists and supports the client but does not fix or caretake.

When we are wisely caring rather than living in the chaos of extremes, we realize we are self-nurturing and self-considerate. This means if we don't spend our lives taking care of others, we can live our lives caring for ourselves. As I said in my book, *Addictive Relationships,* "Without the balancing within the spectrum, our lives become self-destructive and we travel on a compulsive path, destroying our relationship with our own self. If we are not balanced within, we become unbalanced with all of our relationships in general.

## SUGGESTION:
## The Irresponsible/Responsible Capsule

Another way to look at the caretaking-apathy trap is by using the irresponsible/responsible capsule (Figure 7).

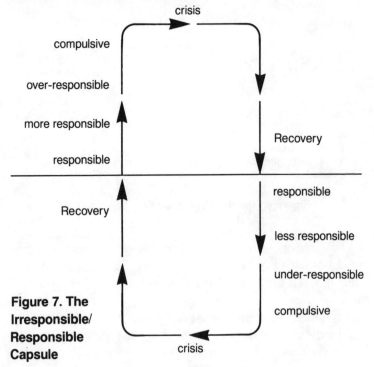

**Figure 7. The Irresponsible/ Responsible Capsule**

As the enabled person takes on less responsibility, the over-responsible person picks up the slack and does more and more to compensate. The cycle quickly becomes a vicious circle of destruction that progresses as we do more and more and more emotionally and physically to make up for the "irresponsible" people in our lives. As a result of our "doing it all," our relationship partner is allowed (or forced) to do less and less and less. Subliminally (sometimes verbally), we suggest he or she is not capable of doing it "right," or perhaps cannot accomplish the mission quickly enough or up to *our* standards. Frustrated with and resentful of the person's inabilities and irresponsibilities, we end up "doing it" ourselves. The relationship is tearing at the seams! We feel hurt and taken for granted, while the irresponsible person sees us as a nagging and dictating perfectionist.

This cycle encourages self-destruction, shame and blame and also promotes low self-esteem for *both* parties. This pattern propagates dependency and spawns addictive relationships. We become resentful and angry at those that we feel mandated to take care of, and find that we act out of obligation instead of love.

*Today I am caring for myself in a way
that illustrates my self-loving capabilities.
I no longer desire to control others' lives,
and realize that my life has been
unmanageable. I am becoming more loving
toward myself and diminishing the hold
that shame played in my past.
I am a beloved child of the universe.
I am enough.*

# 13

# Do You See Yourself As "Not Enough" In Your Basic Core?

He could leap tall buildings in a single bound. He was more powerful than a locomotive and faster than a speeding bullet. But alas, as journalist Clark Kent, Superman's alter ego, he was viewed as "not enough" to be considered as capable. Everyone — including his editor, Perry White — witnessed Clark as a clumsy nerd who somehow always found the daring Superman just as he was foiling a criminal's plot.

As a boy Clark was told never to show his power to others. At his basic core Clark Kent knew he must be masked in illusion or he would not be seen as valuable, worthy and enough. He believed he must cover his true identity or be vulnerable to the world in which he lived.

Despite his miraculous deeds the powerful Superman's ego felt weakness. Kryptonite was his only downfall, and he lived in shame for his powerlessness over the material. Because of this one flaw, Superman felt unmanageable and defectively "human."

So many times we, like Superman, minimize our accomplishments and only witness our self-perceived insecurities, failures and flaws. Believing we are "less than" keeps us locked in shame and pain. We never believe we have done enough. No matter what we do for others with our overresponsible behavior, we believe in our basic core that we are deficient. If we only felt worthy and capable inside we would not need to receive the approval and validation of everyone outside ourselves. If we only felt "enough," then we would not feel so powerless to everyone!

Many of us were bombarded in our dysfunctional homes with one dynamic message that was so shameful and so sinful that it has never been totally appreciated or discussed in recovery literature. Each and every day we were reinforced by an action, word or look that conveyed we were "not enough." Often it was so subliminal we didn't see how it was affecting our very souls. Only in retrospect can we realize its effects on us. In her book, *On Becoming Your Own Parent,* Claudia Black states that we realize only over time that we could not talk about our shame, totally feel our shame, or trust others enough to talk about our shame. The result was we knew we were not enough — we were undeserving and unworthy. Quickly our shame message became a part of each life-sustaining breath. We incorporated this early training into our deepest levels of being. We learned to create a protective system to insulate ourselves from this agonizing, paralyzing realization. We came to believe that we could be enough — if — and only if we took care of everyone else's needs. Surely then people outside ourselves would realize we were capable and deserving.

This shame message of inadequacy was etched deep within our very soul like an open wound that has alienated us from our true self. We lost awareness of our needs, feelings and self-worth. We did not value the words spoken by our inner voice, if we heard them at all.

We were taught to ignore our inner voices and listen only to the needs, wants and desires of others. We thought that making others happy was a means of making ourselves happy. We became alienated from ourselves, chronically unhappy, confused and had difficulty with our relationships.

In my own life I became over-responsible to prove my adequacy and worth. One way I accomplished this was to be co-dependent, the martyr and everyone's victim. I turned over all of my inner strength to everyone else in my life and was confined in a life of blame and guilt. My focus and locus of control was outside myself. I kept my control, I'd never give up my control but gave away my power.

When I became over-responsible and made decisions based on my shame, I allowed outside forces to be my source of power. I believed that if others saw me as giving and loving, then I was assured I possessed the ability to love myself and accept myself completely (then surely we will be enough!).

Entangled in this web of dysfunction is an interesting twist: If I am not enough, then I will surely be abandoned. This cause and effect creates a double-edged blade of pain. If I don't do for others, I will lose them, and if I don't do enough or do it perfectly, I will still lose them. Once again this proves my inadequacy! Either way, my fear of not being enough and fear of abandonment keeps me in a self-destructive cycle of shame, agony and pain.

This is illustrated in the Flow Chart that follows. Other people's needs trigger feelings that make us repeat a behavioral pattern of caretaking and over-responsibility, which eventually proves that we are not good enough. The behavior follows a familiar pattern.

# Stimulus Responsibility
# Flow Chart

pain is correlated into old shame
messages of not being enough
or our fear of abandonment

feelings are triggered
(not always realized)

moment of choice
we may act over-responsible, caretake, fix or
become a martyr

we ignore our own needs and wants, and
respond internally by producing old familiar
behaviors to deal with the pain of the feelings
for relief and release (overeating, addictive
relationships, alcohol usage, controlling,
manipulation, etc.)

our feelings are stuffed inside and we become
emotionally numbed

there is an external payoff for our over-
responsible action (praise, support, appreciation,
affection, etc.)

leads to obsession or compulsion in
relationships, caretaking, increased over-
responsibility, dependency, addictive behaviors

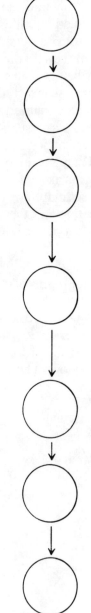

## SUGGESTION:
## 15 Positives

Typically, when a significant person in our life feels "not enough," we encourage them to look at their positive aspects. One method of changing our cycle of destructive patterns is to change our focus by looking at our own positives.

Take a few minutes and write 15 positives about yourself:

_____        _____

_____        _____

_____        _____

_____        _____

_____        _____

_____        _____

_____        _____

_____

## SUGGESTION:
## Fairy Tale Visualization

Try teaming up with a trusted partner to create a story that uses the partner as a hero in a journey that creates a positive conclusion to an unfinished issue. Then read the tale aloud as a meditation/visualization to help heal the shame within.

Tom, for example, created a story of a hero who successfully battled and conquered great odds to discover his inner strength. Forced to battle monsters and an endless maze, the hero still found the strength to survive and go forward. He discovered that the magic gem he was searching out was sewn inside his very coat. Along the way the hero discovered positive elements of his own personhood.

This archetype of the hero who finds what he desires is one useful example of how a fairy tale correlates to our recovery process. Many of us are heros who have not realized we need not rescue others, but must find the strength inside for validation and self-loving.

*Today I find a new direction in my life.*
*I am rejoicing in the progress that I have*
*made and I am deserving of my own love.*
*I am a beloved child of the universe.*
*I am enough.*

14

# Do You Derive Your Self-Worth And Self-Esteem From Sources Outside Yourself?

The familiar music moved us down the street
and into the home that held us enmeshed with
the family that had become part of our own lives.
Edith, Archie, Gloria, and the Meathead were like
members of our own intimate family. We were as
much a part of that family as any of the Bunkers.

The family's over-responsible caretaker was
Edith Bunker. She was an expert at sensing
everyone else's desires but was lost to her own
needs. Her entire world centered around others
— her husband, her daughter, her son-in-law and
her neighbors. Edith's caretaking and
over-responsibility for everyone was the brunt of
many jokes, but we always knew the cruel reality:
Edith had no awareness of her needs or desires.
Unfortunately the only source of our dear friend's
self-esteem was based on the approval and
validation of those around her. She had become
totally camouflaged by her environment through
devaluing her own existence.

Sometimes it seems the universe holds messages for me that repeat themselves over and over. One day my client Joyce stepped into the office. She sat cautiously in the chair, which had represented safety during so many sessions of nurturing and self-loving growth. She looked up with a childlike expression and said, "Joy, I feel like such a prisoner. I want to find my way out." Was the universe filled with this message today? Amazed, I told Joyce to go to the desk and look at what I had been writing. Joyce tentatively stepped to the computer and read:

> "I felt like I was a prisoner in a thick-walled cage," Sue Ellen recalled. "I was hopelessly trapped and felt eternally doomed, knowing that other people had the ability to control me at their will. I felt like a captive in their hands. I realized that sometimes the door opened and closed as others entered my cell, and then for that brief moment there was a possibility for escape. But I felt caught in my corner hiding place, imprisoned and helpless! Shocked by the revelation, I suddenly realized that I myself held the means of escaping from that awful fortress. The key to the prison door was clutched in my own hand. *I* had the means of releasing myself from the horror I experienced all along. *I* was the one who held myself captive!"
>
> Sue Ellen relived her feelings as she closed her eyes and visualized her inner struggle. Her head was lowered and her pain was evident. She lifted her head slowly and told the group about her vision. "I just feel like everything happens to me — *I have no control!* I feel so paralyzed and unable to move . . . things just happen and other people seem to be the decision makers and keepers of my prison sentence. I know that I have a part in this, but it seems like they have much more control of my life than I do."

Joyce and I stood in awkward silence. Suddenly she began to sob, tears spilling down her pale face. "I'm a prisoner too . . . but there are no doors on my prison cell. I have somehow managed to find a way to imprison myself, but I have taken away all the exits. I feel so awful inside. I hurt so much. I must find the way out! Everyone has a piece of me. I try so hard to do it right and be responsible, and it *never*

**The Messages**

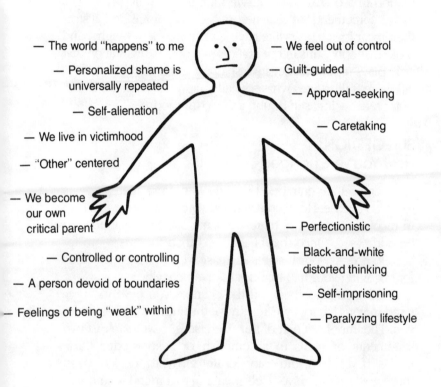

— The world "happens" to me

— Personalized shame is
universally repeated

— Self-alienation

— We live in victimhood

— "Other" centered

— We become
our own
critical parent

— Controlled or controlling

— A person devoid of boundaries

— Feelings of being "weak" within

— We feel out of control

— Guilt-guided

— Approval-seeking

— Caretaking

— Perfectionistic

— Black-and-white
distorted thinking

— Self-imprisoning

— Paralyzing lifestyle

**Figure 8. Low Self-Esteem-Depersonalization**

works out the way I hope. I always feel the shame of not *doing it the way others want it done.* I am a prisoner locked in agonizing shame, over-responsibility and self-destruction."

When we create an environment in which we are surrounded by negativity, we believe that life *happens* to us. We feel powerless and helpless. We begin to internalize all information in a destructive way. We filter all incoming messages as reinforcements of that negative energy force and distort their meanings. This is like having a full-frequency eight-band radio that only pulls in one station — a destructive station that only plays repetitive, negative shame messages.

Figure 8 illustrates what typically happens when we live in outer-referencing, self-doubt, and victimhood.

## SUGGESTION:
### How You've Changed

When you are entrapped in self-destruction, there appears to be no release. Hope comes when you realize your first step in recovery is to admit there are some concerns that need to be addressed. Once that is admitted then there is room for acceptance. As your insights increase, you find new methods for changing your habitual destructive behavior.

Use Figure 9 to check off the changes you have incorporated in your life today. Circle those that are still a concern for you. The important part of this exercise is to write at least two statements or goals to accomplish or acknowledge these issues. If you have difficulty coming up with ideas to meet these goals, imagine yourself speaking to a friend who needs *your* help. What would you suggest your friend do to accomplish these goals?

**Messages**

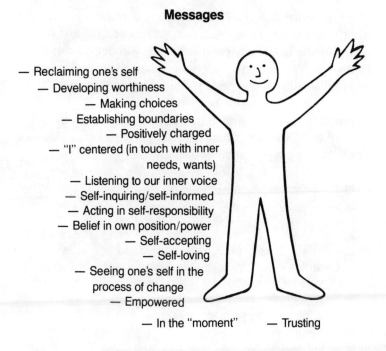

— Reclaiming one's self
— Developing worthiness
— Making choices
— Establishing boundaries
— Positively charged
— "I" centered (in touch with inner
needs, wants)
— Listening to our inner voice
— Self-inquiring/self-informed
— Acting in self-responsibility
— Belief in own position/power
— Self-accepting
— Self-loving
— Seeing one's self in the
process of change
— Empowered

— In the "moment"        — Trusting

**Figure 9. How I've Changed**

## SUGGESTION:
## Visualizing Protection

Visualizations and analogies are amazingly useful and valuable tools in recovery. Many clients discussed the impact of what they witnessed when they saw the movie *Batman* as the Batmobile protected itself from its enemies. The forces, which appeared to be devastating, did not harm the elusive black vehicle. Prepared for any attack, the Batmobile protected itself with a cocoon of interlocking shields that proved impregnable. With remarkable ease this protective armor kept every onslaught from penetrating the vulnerable target.

You have the ability to protect yourself in the same fashion when you lovingly take yourself in your own arms and accept who you are. Unfortunately many times you discover that evil forces can come from your inner shame, as well as from external assailants. You need to learn to protect yourself from your own "negative wizards."

You can visualize that impenetrable protection in many creative ways. One visualization that I use regularly involves a loving, supportive protection system:

> Imagine a giant, loving white bandage that encircles your entire body with protection and love. Feel the gauze slowly wind and wrap each part of your body gently and protectively. Feel the warmth, the security, the safety. Feel it move around each part of your body as it accepts each part of you and embraces you. Let this warmth create an environment that fosters the growth of inner love. Envision this white wrap like a warm, cuddly cocoon protecting you from negative messages and all the potential harm in your life. This is your safe place . . . nothing can harm you when you are with your inner child! Feel the warm healing glow as you nurture yourself and embrace your child. It feels like the safety of a womb. You are the child and the mother together caring for yourself as you always desired. You are insulated within your own safe home of love and security.

This cocooning process is a loving, care-giving — not care-taking — means of reparenting our inner wounded child. As you discover your power to heal your shame, you nurture the child inside who has been locked deep within your being. Move within and see that your focus for change is within you. All that you need, all of your miracles, are inside! You do not need to caretake others to feel worthy. You can create a means to feel worthy. You do not need to be over-responsible for others. Be self-responsible and give yourself the love that you desperately need.

*As I reclaim myself I discover what I have always held. I learn to be self-caring and loving and find the gifts that I had locked away for safekeeping. I am a beloved child of the universe. I am enough.*

## 15

# Do You Believe That The Best Way To Get Something Done Is To Do It Yourself?

To boldly go where no man has gone before:
The voyages of the Starship *Enterprise* moved us
into unknown galaxies. Their ten-year mission
encouraged the crew to accomplish the Starfleet's
goal of seeking new life forms and establishing
communication, while protecting all of the life
forms. Only they could manage to bring peace
and protection to all they encountered.

Captain Kirk (surely an over-responsible first
child) and Mr. Spock (a child of a dysfunctional
Vulcan family who learned to shut down all of his
human emotions to perfection), appeared to take
responsibility for fixing every situation that
affected the universe. Their co-dependent
behavior was in the interest of the common good,
but many times they did not allow the inhabitants
of the universe to proceed in their own recovery
at *their* own pace. They believed they were the
superior life forms in the galaxy (the keepers of
truth, honesty and honor) and forged on in their
mission to save the worlds!

Recovery involves risk. Allowing ourselves the opportunity to look at what is hiding deep inside is probably the most fearful risk of all. Our over-responsibility, perfectionism and caretaking have always been a means of controlling the world around us. If we focus on others, we do not have to face ourselves! We always believed that if we could control the outside environment, the inside (the inner child) would be controlled and "enough." Then maybe we would be lovable? Gerald Jampolsky, in *Love Is Letting Go Of Fear*, states,

> "It might be helpful to question our need to attempt to control the external world. We can, instead consistently control our inner world by choosing what thoughts we want to hand to our mind. Peace of mind begins with our own thoughts and extends outward. It is from our peace of mind that a peaceful perception of [our] the world arises."

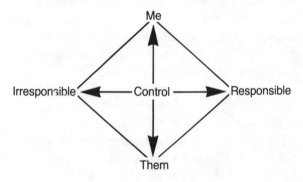

**Figure 10. What Is Mine?**

## SUGGESTION:
## What Is Mine?

When any situation arises, I typically see an opportunity to be responsible and act capably. My actions center around a way to control my environment by being helpful and giving to others. I feel that my responsible action allows me to feel balanced with my control of the destiny. I can feel useful and needed when I am the responsible one. In this way I know I will be totally in charge of all the options as well as the consequences. As long as I am in control, I am quite capable of "handling" all circumstances, even if there are consequences. Being responsible means being willing to put myself on the line and take on the shame that I will bring to myself if the situation does not work. Either way, success or failure, I know that I will be able to handle the situation and will not have to rely on anyone else. (It is always easier for me to take on the blame rather than delegate or make others responsible for their actions).

By allowing another person to be self-responsible, the over-responsible person must surrender control. This creates uncertainty for the outcome and loss for control over the result. "Doing it all" allows you the opportunity to "be enough," to gain validation and approval, and to feel like you can manage your destiny!

You can learn to look at some other options in your life by using the following chart in any given circumstance:

| What is mine? | What is his/hers? |
| --- | --- |
|  |  |

This is anyone's territory

**Figure 10a. Mine And Yours**

## SUGGESTION:
## What Would Happen If . . . ?

What would happen if you did not rescue or be over-responsible for a situation?

_____

_____

_____

_____

What might be the positives if you allow someone else to handle a situation?

_____

_____

_____

_____

What is your fear if you do not do things yourself?

_____

_____

_____

_____

*The gift of self-awareness is what
I desire in my life. I am willing to
discover my gifts and celebrate my
wonderment. I am a beloved child
of the universe. I am enough.*

# Word Games

Words are powerful tools that express our experiences, feelings and joy. But words have different meanings for each of us. Many times our mental filtering of words and their meanings trigger internal shame messages. This may be completely in opposition, or at least in contrast, to the intent of the words spoken by our spouses, significant others, friends or family.

As you read the following words notice what stirs inside when you think about their meaning in your life. Do you think of pain? Abuse? Does a word bring a lump to your throat?

Each word has been broken in order to help you hear it in a new way. I hope these little words will help you visualize concepts in a new way along your path.

*CON-TROL:* Sometimes we believe it is necessary to "con" to attain the control we need so that we may take charge of a situation. Our manipulation may be subliminal and unconscious, but many times we need to use drastic measures to feel in control of our lives. It is understandable that we have a need to control the people, places and things around us because we had no control as children. But it is quite evident that this drive to control has become a vicious cycle of self-destruction. We have come to realize, that no matter how much we "con," we are only fooling ourselves. The notion that we are capable of controlling others is an illusion. One group member looked at the word "control" and said it reminded him of "troll" under a bridge. This ugly troll tries to "con" people into liking him. Eventually the troll learns people will like him without the manipulation and trickery when he is authentic and real. That acceptance will happen when you are real and authentic with yourself.

*OVER-RESPONSE-ABILITY:* A lot of tricks in this word! First of all the word implies that we respond. That is not quite accurate. We don't *respond* (which suggests that we take into account our needs, wants and desires, after which a decision is made based upon choices); but we usually have *reactions*. A reaction means that we act out of our need for approval, desire to fix, or need to attain love and acceptance. We discover that a stimulus demands attention to which we must react. Many times we lose ourselves in the process and completely ignore our personal inner guide. Perhaps it should be called over-reaction-ability.

*RESPONSE-ABILITY:* Now there is a phrase that does make a lot of sense! When we use the abilities we command to look within, we do make responses (versus reactions). We discover that we are balanced and can therefore make healthy response-abilities.

*BL-AM-E and SH-AM-E:* Both words have the middle letters of "am." Shame and blame say something about us as people. It says to us that something is wrong with us: I am bad. I am no good. I am not enough. When we accept and change shame messages in recovery, we will learn to accept and love the "am" inside.

*RE-SENT-MENT:* Whenever we have resentments we cannot release, we find that our anger is *sent* back to us! Anger is like a hot, burning coal. As Buddha said, when we pick it up to throw it at another, we burn ourselves. Pain and anguish are surely sent back to their origins when we do not constructively process our anger.

*E-NO-UGH:* No, we never believe we have done it right (perfectionism). We search the universe to find the magic which will make us what we want to be for others or ourselves. When we listen to our Higher Power we discover inner power and love. We are enough when we say *no* to the habits which result in mental destruction.

*F-EAR:* Fear talks compulsively into our *ears* (not quietly, mind you), telling us that we are not capable. Fear tells us we have to worry that others will leave us if we don't hold them up. Fear tells us we are not enough and we are not complete. Fear cripples and results in the holocaust of the body, mind and spirit.

This reminds me of a story Rokelle Lerner uses in her workshops. She speaks of the "audience" that sits on her shoulder. This group consists of voices from her mother, father, siblings, teachers and friends. When we listen to fear, we *hear* these voices. When we listen to ourselves, we *hear* love and feel strength. It is time to put new messages in our ears and train our ears to acknowledge their gentle, hopeful words!

*RE-COVER-Y:* As we move into the Light, we discover that we have lived with covers over our eyes, shrouding the feelings within our hearts. As we begin to care for ourselves and find the love we hold inside, we throw off all the entrapping covers and veils holding us back. Our child within is healing love as we learn how to nurture that little one that lives within us all!

Many people say that you can't *recover* what you never had. Truly that is a misconception. You may never have known the skills but have harbored an inner strength all along, comprised of many positive, loving elements. As you grow in recovery you will find your path being guided by many forms of self-nurturing.

*L-I-GHT:* As we learn to focus on the "I" within, we feel the Light of inner love and we learn to be self-considerate and loving. We learn to love others through facilitation, support and encouragement (versus caretaking, enabling and being over-responsible). This process allows us to encourage others' growth as we enhance our own despite the fact that upon first glance, we can perceive this inward focus as selfish.

*A-BAN-DONMENT:* When we fear abandonment, we try to prohibit (ban) or forbid others from leaving us. We believe this ban on their free choice will keep us safe. But we actually prohibit our own growth as we attempt to restrict others.

*PURR-FECTIONISM:* Our hope is that life will *purr* like a cat who is totally content. But for many of us this tranquility appears to be an illusive commodity. The more we try to control and be perfect, the more we torment the raging bull inside of us. Perfectionism is an obsession of the mind because it results in continual failure.

*CARE-TAKE:* When we do things for others we find that we *take* away their power. If we do not allow ourselves to be caring (versus caretaking) without controlling and being responsible, ultimately, we will *take* away others' lessons.

*WORTH-LESS:* When we feel worthless, we feel we are worth less than others in our lives. The erroneous conclusion is because we are not "enough" and worth less. But as we journey into recovery, we discover we are *worthy* of our own love.

*EN-MESH-MENT:* A *mesh* is a means of catching or holding something fast. We think we can catch or hold something when we are enmeshed. Typically what we catch in the mesh is the fantasy of wishing things would come out differently. We get so caught up in the mesh we emerge a real mess!

Look at the word again. If you look inside the word and take note of the letters and switch them around you find the words *he, she,* and *me.* When we are enmeshed, we get messed up in all types and forms of relationships with people.

*I am enough just as I am right now.*
*I am whole. I am complete.*
*I am a beloved child of the universe*
*and I am healing the over-responsibility*
*and shame that once held me back!*

# Epilogue

*The deeper the sorrow comes
into your being,
the more joy it can contain.*

*— Kahlil Gibran*

With each day I am learning skills to help me release and surrender the hold of my over-responsible patterns. Only I have the power to heal my shame and bring joy into my life. I know the key is to release others with love so they may be responsible for their destiny. In this process I release myself from the burdens of controlling. I have found freedom and serenity along the path.

The pain and sorrow of my over-responsibility has cut deep into my shame-based existence, but now I realize what a miracle I am in my recovery. Today I know what joy is contained inside. Celebrate your progress as we discover our joy within!

## Conclusion:

Together we have come into new insights. Awareness is the first step toward integrating new behaviors. Celebrate your process, and love yourself each time you witness a risk or a change along your pathway. Too often we get trapped in the "work" of recovery and ignore the joyous renewal of our freedom from shame. Take time to love yourself — you *are* a beloved child of the universe and a miracle to behold.

With Light And Love
Joy

# Recommended Reading

Becker, Robert. **Addicted To Misery: The Other Side Of Co-dependency.** Deerfield Beach, FL: Health Communications, 1989.

Black, Claudia. **It Will Never Happen To Me.** Denver, CO: M.A.C., Printing and Publications Div., 1982.

Wills-Brandon, Carla. **Learning To Say No: Establishing Healthy Boundaries.** Deerfield Beach, FL: Health Communications, 1990.

_____ **Is It Love Or Is It Sex? Why Relationships Don't Work.** Deerfield Beach, FL: Health Communications, 1989.

Castine, Jackie. **Recovery From Rescuing.** Deerfield Beach, FL: Health Communications, 1989.

Fishel, Ruth. **The Journey Within: A Spiritual Path To Recovery.** Deerfield Beach, FL: Health Communications, 1987.

_____ **Learning To Live In The Now: 6 Week Personal Plan To Recovery.** Deerfield Beach, FL: Health Communications, 1988.

_____ **Time For Joy: Daily Affirmations.** Deerfield Beach, FL: Health Comunications, 1988.

Fossom, Merle A. and Mason, Marilyn J. **Facing Shame: Families in Recovery.** New York: W.W. Norton, 1986.

Gawain, Shakti and King, Laurel. **Living In The Light.** San Rafael, CA: New World Library, 1986.

Hay, Louise. **You Can Heal Your Life.** Santa Monica, CA: Hay House, 1984.

Jaffe, Dennis T. and Scott, Cynthia D. **From Burnout To Balance: A Workbook for Personal Self-Renewal.** New York: McGraw, 1984.

Kritsberg, Wayne. **Adult Children of Alcoholics Syndrome: From Discovery to Recovery.** Pompano Beach, FL: Health Communications, 1986.

_____ **Healing Together: A Guide To Intimacy and Recovery For Co-dependent Couples.** Deerfield Beach, FL: Health Communications, 1990.

Larsen, Earnie. **Stage II Recovery.** Minneapolis, MN: Winston Press, 1985.

Lee, John. **I Don't Want To Be Alone.** Deerfield Beach, FL: Health Communications, 1990.

_____ **The Flying Boy: Healing The Wounded Man.** Deerfield Beach, FL: Health Communications, 1987.

Lerner, Rokelle. **Daily Affirmations For Adult Children of Alcoholics.** Pompano Beach, FL: Health Communications, 1985.

_____ **Affirmations For The Inner Child.** Deerfield Beach, FL: Health Communications, 1990.

MacLaine, Shirley. **Out On A Limb.** Toronto: Bantam Books, 1983.

Middelton-Moz, Jane. **Shame and Guilt: Masters of Disguise.** Deerfield Beach, FL: Health Communications, 1990.

_____ **Children of Trauma.** Deerfield Beach, FL: Health Communications, 1989.

Miller, Joy and Marianne Ripper. **Following The Yellow Brick Road: The Adult Child's Personal Journey Through Oz.** Pompano Beach, FL: Health Communications, 1988.

Miller, Joy. **Addictive Relationships: Reclaiming Your Boundaries.** Deerfield Beach, FL: Health Communications, 1989.

Rodegast, Pat and Stanton, Judith. **Emmanuel's Book: A Manual For Living Comfortably in the Cosmos.** New York: Bantam, 1985.

Viscott, David. **Risking.** New York: Simon & Schuster, 1977.

Whaley, D. **Being Your Own Parent.** New York: Doubleday, 1988.

# Daily Affirmation Books from . . .
# Health Communications

*GENTLE REMINDERS FOR CO-DEPENDENTS: Daily Affirmations*
Mitzi Chandler

With insight and humor, Mitzi Chandler takes the co-dependent and the adult child through the year. Gentle Reminders is for those in recovery who seek to enjoy the miracle each day brings.

ISBN 1-55874-020-1                                                              $6.95

*TIME FOR JOY: Daily Affirmations*
Ruth Fishel

With quotations, thoughts and healing energizing affirmations these daily messages address the fears and imperfections of being human, guiding us through self-acceptance to a tangible peace and the place within where there is *time for joy.*

ISBN 0-932194-82-6                                                              $6.95

*AFFIRMATIONS FOR THE INNER CHILD*
Rokelle Lerner

This book contains powerful messages and helpful suggestions aimed at adults who have unfinished childhood issues. By reading it daily we can end the cycle of suffering and move from pain into recovery.

ISBN 1-55874-045-6                                                              $6.95

*DAILY AFFIRMATIONS: For Adult Children of Alcoholics*
Rokelle Lerner

Affirmations are a way to discover personal awareness, growth and spiritual potential, and self-regard. Reading this book gives us an opportunity to nurture ourselves, learn who we are and what we want to become.

ISBN 0-932194-47-3
(Little Red Book)                                                              $6.95
(New Cover Edition)                                                            $6.95

*SOOTHING MOMENTS: Daily Meditations For Fast-Track Living*
Bryan E. Robinson, Ph.D.

This is designed for those leading fast-paced and high-pressured lives who need time out each day to bring self-renewal, joy and serenity into their lives.

ISBN 1-55874-075-9                                                              $6.95

3201 S.W. 15th Street,
Deerfield Beach, FL 33442
1-800-851-9100

**Health Communications, Inc.**